T0304387

FATAL
FORECAST

AN INCREDIBLE TRUE STORY OF
COURAGE IN A SAVAGE STORM

BY MICHAEL J. TOUGIAS

TRUE SURVIVAL SERIES

Abandon Ship!
(cowritten with Alison O'Leary)

Fatal Forecast

TRUE RESCUE SERIES

The Finest Hours

A Storm Too Soon

Into the Blizzard

Attacked at Sea
(cowritten with Alison O'Leary)

In Harm's Way
(Young Readers Adaptation of Doug Stanton's
In Harm's Way)

Rescue of the Bounty

TRUE SURVIVAL SERIES

FATAL FORECAST

AN INCREDIBLE TRUE STORY OF
COURAGE IN A SAVAGE STORM

MICHAEL J. TOUGIAS

Christy Ottaviano Books
LITTLE, BROWN AND COMPANY
New York Boston

Christy Ottaviano Books
Hachette Book Group
1290 Avenue of the Americas, New York, NY 10104
Visit us at LBYR.com

First Edition: October 2024

Christy Ottaviano Books is an imprint of Little, Brown and Company. The Christy Ottaviano Books name and logo are registered trademarks of Hachette Book Group, Inc.

The publisher is not responsible for websites (or their content) that are not owned by the publisher.

Little, Brown and Company books may be purchased in bulk for business, educational, or promotional use. For information, please contact your local bookseller or the Hachette Book Group Special Markets Department at special.markets@hbgusa.com.

Library of Congress Cataloging-in-Publication Data
Names: Tougias, Michael J., 1955– author.
Title: Fatal forecast : an incredible true story of courage in a savage storm / Michael J. Tougias.
Description: First edition. | New York ; Boston : Little, Brown and Company, [2024] | Series: True survival series ; Book 2 | "*Fatal Forecast: An Incredible True Story of Courage in a Savage Storm* was adapted for young readers by Michael J. Tougias. It is an abridgment of the adult book *Fatal Forecast: An Incredible True Tale of Disaster and Survival at Sea* by Michael J. Tougias, originally published in 2007 by Scribner, a division of Simon & Schuster" —Copyright page. | Includes bibliographical references. | Audience: Ages 9–14 years | Summary: "A spellbinding, moment-by-moment account of seventy-two hours in the lives of eight young fishermen—some of whom would never set foot on dry land again—as they fight to survive a deadly storm in the middle of winter." —Provided by publisher.
Identifiers: LCCN 2023050190 | ISBN 9780316556217 (hardcover) | ISBN 9780316556415 (ebook)
Subjects: LCSH: Shipwrecks—Georges Bank. | Survival at sea—Georges Bank. | Fair Wind (Lobster boat) | Sea Fever (Lobster boat) | Lobster fishers—Massachusetts—Cape Cod. | Storms—New England.
Classification: LCC G530 .F1269 2024 | DDC 910.9163/45—dc23/eng/20231201
LC record available at https://lccn.loc.gov/2023050190

ISBNs: 978-0-316-55621-7 (hardcover), 978-0-316-55641-5 (ebook)

Printed in Indiana, USA

LSC-C, 03/25

Printing 2, 2025

TO JILL PORTER AND THE CREWS OF THE
FAIR WIND, SEA FEVER, **AND** *BROADBILL*

DAVE BERRY

BRAD BOWEN

GARY BROWN

PETER BROWN

BILLY GARNOS

ERNIE HAZARD

GRANT MOORE

RICHARD ROWELL

ROB THAYER

CONTENTS

PART III

VESSELS, AIRCRAFT, AND CREW

PRIMARY CHARACTERS AND VESSELS

Fair Wind (fifty-foot lobster boat)
> **Billy Garnos,** captain
> **Rob Thayer,** crew member
> **Dave Berry,** crew member
> **Ernie Hazard,** crew member
> **Charlie Raymond,** owner

Sea Fever (forty-seven-foot lobster boat)
> **Peter Brown,** captain
> **Gary Brown,** crew member
> **Richard "Sarge" Rowell,** crew member
> **Brad Bowen,** crew member

Sea Star (seventy-foot lobster boat)
> **Bob Brown,** owner and captain
> **Mike Sosnowski,** crew member

Broadbill (sixty-five-foot lobster boat)
> **Grant Moore,** captain

Maria Pavlis, fiancée of Billy Garnos

Givens life raft (attached to *Fair Wind*)

A six-foot-diameter life raft with a dome-shaped canopy. A survivor could enter the raft through a small doorway in the canopy. An empty bag, called a ballast bag, hung beneath the raft so that seawater could fill it and stabilize the raft, helping it stay upright when hit by waves. If the ballast bag was torn, the life raft could flip like any other raft. A supply bag inside the raft contained a hand pump to add air to the raft, a knife, canned water and an opener, and a tin of cookies. The life raft was orange to make it easier to spot by aircraft searching the ocean.

OTHER CHARACTERS, VESSELS, AND AIRCRAFT

Active (210-foot Coast Guard cutter)

Carl Helman, captain

Dave Nicholson, operations officer

Tommy Dutton, crew member

Bill Gatter, radio operator

Wayne Hennessy, quartermaster

Active (twenty-six-foot launch)

Tom McKenzie, crew member

HH-3F helicopter

Buck Baley, pilot

Joe Touzin, pilot

Tony Davern, navigator

P-3 Orion (naval long-range patrol plane)

Craig Martin, radio operator

At Coast Guard regional headquarters in Boston

Robert Eccles, lieutenant

PROLOGUE

GEORGES BANK, LOCATED ONE HUNDRED MILES EAST
of Cape Cod, Massachusetts, is one of the richest fishing grounds in the world. It is an oval-shaped plateau
on the ocean's floor, roughly the size of Massachusetts, Rhode Island, and Connecticut combined. Sixteen thousand years ago, during the ice age, Georges
Bank was land, not sea, a broad coastal plain connected to the rest of North America. Nearby Nantucket and Martha's Vineyard were the largest hills in
the region. As the glaciers melted and retreated, water
filled in the deeper channels around Georges Bank,
making it an island. Trapped on this enormous island
were land animals such as woolly mammoths, mas-
todons, moose, and caribou, whose teeth are today
sometimes brought up in fishing nets. As the sea rose,
more of the island flooded, and roughly six thousand
years ago all of it was submerged.

Water depths on Georges Bank are irregular; in

some places canyons plunge thousands of feet deep. In other sections shoals of sand rise to within ten feet of the ocean's surface. Such shallow waters have led to exaggerated tales of fishermen claiming to have played baseball in ankle-deep water during low tide. The shoals are the very reason fishermen venture onto the Bank. Rays of sunlight can reach the bottom, allowing plankton to grow. Small fish gather to feed on the plankton, and larger fish in turn prey on them.

The Bank's tremendous currents also contribute to the fishery by creating a high-energy environment of cycling nutrients and oxygen. These currents, a swirling combination of tidal and surface waves, produce a constant turbulence when they collide over the sandy shoals.

Many of the first fishermen to visit the Bank never went back, fearing the currents were too strong for them to safely anchor their boats. One early fisherman recounted a grim story of what happens when an anchor cable snaps. He was on board an anchored vessel in a storm when another boat, whose anchor had broken loose, careened past. "The drifting vessel was coming directly at us.... With the swiftness of a gull she passed by, so near that I could have leaped aboard....The hopeless, terror-stricken faces of the crew we saw but a moment." The doomed ship then struck another vessel, and both went down.

Georges Bank is also dangerous because of its location in the Atlantic. On the eastern end of the Bank the warm waters of the Gulf Stream collide with the cold Labrador Current, creating swirling waves. Although the currents at Georges Bank are almost always rough, when strong winds are added, chaotic seas occur. Fishermen who venture out to Georges Bank need a boat large and sturdy enough to handle these seas. Help, should you need it, is hours away, an eternity if your vessel is going down. Captains fishing Georges Bank understand this, and the smart ones keep their boats in tip-top shape and always have one ear glued to the radio, listening to each and every updated weather report. If a big storm is coming, they get out of its way—fast.

Year upon year, boats have a way of disappearing on Georges Bank. Even with radios, many vessels that sink give no indication of their coming doom. Something sudden and catastrophic happens, and the boat sinks within seconds, joining the hundreds of others on the bottom.

The deadly nature of Georges Bank is the trade-off fishermen must reckon with to get at catches richer than those found closer to shore. To fish the Bank one must accept the risk. This is not an environment for the fainthearted. The men who work the Bank are a rugged lot, who quickly develop a certain toughness that keeps fear in check. One of these men was thirty-three-year-old Ernie Hazard. What he endured on Georges Bank is nothing short of remarkable.

Part I

Chapter 1

THE *FAIR WIND* CREW

ERNIE HAZARD WAS IN HIS THIRD YEAR OF OFFSHORE lobster fishing, and although the work was brutally demanding, he felt fortunate. The *Fair Wind*, a fifty-foot steel lobster boat on which Ernie worked, was a meticulously maintained vessel equipped with the most modern gear and electronics. Equally important, Ernie enjoyed the company of his fellow crew members and his captain. No one slacked off, and everyone contributed to making the *Fair Wind* a very profitable boat.

On November 20, 1980, the crew was having dinner at the Backside Saloon in Hyannis, Massachusetts, enjoying a good meal before making the last trip of the season. The men had made close to thirty fishing trips to Georges Bank since the previous April. They were all looking forward to having the next four months off. Ernie talked about going down to Florida to see his brother or possibly heading out to Carmel, California, to visit friends. Thirty-year-old captain Billy Garnos planned to focus on his new house and his fiancée, Maria. Rob Thayer, age twenty-two, hadn't made any definite plans, but he hoped to travel, having spent prior offseasons in such far-flung places as the Canadian province of New-foundland and Labrador. Dave Berry, the youngest crew member at just twenty years old, lived up in Marblehead, Massachusetts, and he'd likely take a lit-tle time off to be with friends.

Ernie felt relaxed that night, quietly listening as the rest of the crew discussed their plans. Every now and then he made a joke or a wry comment. The oth-ers had come to enjoy his humor and quick, dry wit. They also appreciated the muscle and stamina packed into his burly six-foot frame. He had arms as big as most men's thighs, and he put those arms to good use hauling and setting lobster traps. He looked tough and perhaps a bit menacing with his muscular arms, piercing black eyes, and wild black beard, but his crewmates knew that behind the gruff exterior was an intelligent and thoughtful man.

Although Ernie was the oldest of the crew at age thirty-three, the others had been fishing just as long or longer. Ernie got his position on board the *Fair Wind* by simply answering a help wanted ad he'd seen in the newspaper three years earlier. He was single and living in Peabody, Massachusetts, bouncing from one factory job to another. When Ernie saw the advertisement for a crewman, he was between jobs, so he figured, *What the heck, that's something I've never done.*

The boat's owner, Charlie Raymond, worked alongside Billy Garnos and another crew member, so Ernie became the fourth crewman. Ernie had never been offshore, and on his first trip out he couldn't help but think that he had entered another world as he gazed at the gray ocean stretching endlessly in all directions.

Some newcomers to commercial fishing get spooked and disoriented on their initial voyage when they realize how insignificant their boat is compared to the enormous ocean. But Ernie was fascinated by the new experience. Charlie Raymond and Billy Garnos kept him busy from the moment he set foot on the *Fair Wind*, teaching him everything they could.

"They had me driving the boat," says Ernie, "which was a big deal for me. I'd never driven a fifty-foot boat, and I loved every minute of it. Plowing through that vast open space was a thrill, and I remember thinking this is absolutely incredible."

Ernie's initial trip on the *Fair Wind* was also the boat's first of the season. When they reached the fishing grounds after a twenty-hour ride, Ernie learned what it took to make a living from the sea. "I wondered how long these people were going to work without taking a rest," says Ernie. "They seemed tireless."

The boat was loaded with dozens of traps, and they had to bait each one and then drop it down. There were twenty-two traps to a trawl (a set or string of traps), and on that trip they dropped three trawls. They worked throughout the day and well into the night. As backbreaking as the work seemed, the next trip was even tougher. The crew had to haul in the previously set traps, rebait them, then drop them over again.

Ernie's hands had not yet developed calluses, and

his tender flesh was in constant pain from pulling so much rope. He found he had muscles in his hands and forearms that he'd never felt before, and they ached incessantly. But he didn't complain. He enjoyed the ocean setting and the guys who worked beside him.

The trips fell into a pattern of five days out at sea, and then a day or two back in port. Ernie's skin quickly developed thick calluses, and the muscles in his hands became so large he could barely touch his thumb to his smallest finger. Charlie and Billy continued to teach him about the boat and lobstering. Ernie soaked up as much as he could, enthralled by this new ocean world. Each trip was different. Sometimes the North Atlantic unleashed an angry series of pounding waves, but other times the water remained as smooth as glass, and from the surface the crew could tell the difference between a swordfish and a shark almost a mile away.

Ernie's pay depended on the catch, and sometimes they just caught a few lobsters. On one trip the only thing caught in the trap was a lobster claw, but what a claw it was. It measured seventeen inches long and contained fifteen pounds of meat. Ernie kept the claw, removed the meat, lacquered the shell, and mounted it at his mother's home to show friends who couldn't believe its size. The lobster from which the claw had come likely measured five feet from the tail to the outstretched claw.

During Ernie's second year, owner Charlie Raymond made Billy Garnos the captain so that Charlie could concentrate on the construction of a bigger boat. Billy, an unusually generous young man who had bought a home and invited his parents and grandmother to live with him, proved an able skipper. Charlie promised Billy that when the bigger boat was ready, it would be his to captain.

Unlike some commercial fishermen who blew half their weekly paychecks the first day they were back in port, Billy saved a good portion of his. It was this maturity and sense of loyalty that caught the eye of Charlie Raymond, and Charlie knew he had just the kind of man he wanted to captain his boat.

Rob Thayer and Dave Berry rounded out the rest of the crew, and all of them had great respect and confidence in Billy as their captain. The four men had formed a tight bond, and they often chose to have dinner together before setting out to sea.

For Rob Thayer, this was his first season aboard

the *Fair Wind*, but after the steep learning curve of the first few weeks, he was now pulling his weight just like the others. Rob and Dave Berry, both in their early twenties, formed a quick friendship. Dave was an experienced deckhand, having worked on the ocean since he was fifteen. He too saved a good deal of his fishing pay and had just bought a new pickup truck.

Young, confident, and hardworking, the crew seemingly had their whole lives in front of them.

———

Now, as the four men ate and talked at the Backside Saloon, they knew the upcoming week at Georges Bank would be a cold one. Late-November temperatures could be expected to hover in the 40s and 50s during the day and drop lower at night. Still, the more important factors were the wind and whether or not storms were forecast for the region. Whenever Billy learned of an approaching storm before a late-season trip, he'd delay departure until the storm passed. Georges Bank in November could be a very nasty place, and it was not the time of year to take chances.

The next morning, the men met at sunrise and

prepared the boat for the final trip, stowing food, bait, and gear. The old fisherman's superstition that it's bad luck to leave on a Friday did not deter the crew and never had. Men like Ernie and Billy felt that if you put stock in superstitions, you'd never get any fishing done. The crew of the *Fair Wind* felt no sense of foreboding that day, no ominous premonitions.

As he'd done the night before, Billy listened to the National Weather Service forecast for Georges Bank. The forecast called for southeast winds of fifteen to twenty-five knots (or about 1.15 miles per hour), shifting to northwest at twenty to thirty knots at night, followed by similar conditions for Saturday with some rain and fog. Seas would be three to six feet Friday and five to ten feet on Saturday. The report was quite typical for Georges Bank, and the crew of the *Fair Wind* had no reason to doubt its accuracy.

One of the key components of forecasting weather at sea is the information obtained from weather buoys. The weather buoys transmit hourly reports on sea level pressure, air temperature, sea surface temperature, wave height, and the all-important wind speed and direction.

On that day, however, the Georges Bank buoy

was malfunctioning. And just to the north, the Gulf of Maine buoy was not even afloat, but was on land being repaired. Thus, the weather report was based on incomplete data. The management at the National Weather Service, which is part of the National Oceanic and Atmospheric Administration, had known about the situation for months. They had elected not to alert mariners of the problem.

Billy Garnos, Ernie Hazard, Rob Thayer, and Dave Berry headed out to sea based on what they believed to be the same reliable forecasts they had grown to trust over the years. They looked forward to a smooth trip.

But on that November day, the *Fair Wind* was on a collision course with a storm that produced waves more monstrous than anything the crew had ever seen.

Chapter 2

HEADING OUT

ERNIE HAZARD GREW UP IN COCHITUATE, MASSA-
chusetts, located about twenty miles west of Boston.
Although he didn't spend much time near the ocean,
he loved the water, particularly Dudley Pond and
nearby swamps.

He and his brothers would spend hours on end
fishing for horned pout and pickerel and catching
frogs and turtles.

Ernie's father died when he was fifteen, and Ernie,
who was already independent-minded and stub-
born, spent more time in the swamps and less time at
school. At the beginning of his senior year his mother
remarried, and she and her husband moved to Peabody, but Ernie refused to go. Instead he got a job at a

gas station near Cochituate. He went to school during the day and pumped gas in the evening. At night he slept inside the garage of the gas station. When school officials discovered this, they forced him out of school because he didn't have a parent living in the town, and Ernie reluctantly joined his mother in Peabody.

Just before graduating from high school, Ernie was drafted, and he entered the army in November 1965. He was trained in mechanics and within a few months found himself serving in Korea. One would think that a freewheeling teenager would rebel against army life. Ernie, however, didn't mind the rigors of the service, and he loved the experience of traveling overseas. When his service was over he returned to Peabody and landed a job at the nearby General Electric plant.

He took a year off from working to tour the West Coast. Determined not to be a passive tourist, he decided to travel the back roads, under his own power, and alone. He hitchhiked to Washington State, bought a bicycle, and pedaled south on a three-month odyssey. He didn't stop until he reached Mexico.

When Ernie joined the crew of the *Fair Wind*, he bonded quickly with his crewmates because in many ways they were a lot like him: tough, independent,

and up for new adventures. While friends were set-
tling down in nine-to-five jobs, these men were out
on the ocean from April through November, working eighteen-hour days. In those eight months at sea
the goal was simple: make as much money as possible so that during the winter months they could do
whatever they pleased.

This freedom was made possible by a bottom-
dwelling crustacean with a greenish-brown shell,
the lobster. These ancient, armored creatures have
two huge specialized claws. The right one acts as a
pincher, and the slightly larger left claw is used as a
crusher. With these powerful tools lobsters catch and
crush both living and dead organisms, including fish,
sea worms, mollusks, and small crustaceans. They are
also cannibalistic, attacking smaller members of their
own species.

Lobster habitat is often found in shallow, craggy
coastal areas. But these creatures can also live in
depths in excess of two thousand feet and are particularly abundant in the submarine canyons of Georges
Bank. These offshore lobsters travel more extensively
than their coastal cousins, often covering as many as
180 miles during spring migrations.

Prior to the 1950s, offshore lobsters were usually incidental catches in nets intended for other fish. Fishermen knew there were plenty of lobsters in the canyons and in the holes of the canyon walls, but conventional traps and nets were inefficient at capturing them. In the late 1950s, however, technological advances in trap design and hauling allowed fishermen to work the deep waters.

Georges Bank lobsters were also considerably larger than those found inshore, with some reaching twenty pounds or more. Offshore lobstering brought better yields than inshore, and boats like the *Fair Wind* found less competition from other lobstermen when they were out as far as Georges Bank. The bigger paydays, however, were not without a risk: should trouble strike, aid could be a long way off.

The crew of the *Fair Wind* used large wooden traps, each weighing about 125 pounds. When the traps were lifted, the crewmen removed the lobsters, keeping the legal ones and throwing the undersized back into the sea. The crewmen took turns banding the lobsters and either rebaiting and lowering the traps or stacking them for placement in another area. Each man was lifting, sliding, and slinging tons of gear in a single day, and stacking the traps in rough seas was perhaps the most difficult of all the duties.

Working with heavy, cumbersome gear on a moving deck takes strength and athleticism. Endurance was, and still is, the primary attribute needed in a lobster fisherman. Every offshore boat aims to maximize its catch in as little time as possible. The goal of the *Fair Wind*'s crew was to get on and off the fishing grounds as quickly as possible, so the men put in seventeen to twenty hours of work each day.

As the *Fair Wind* left Hyannis around noon on Friday, November 21, the crew took two-hour shifts at the wheel. Driving the boat to the fishing grounds was the least demanding part of the trip, consisting of looking out the window for other boats and watching the radar. Dave Berry manned the wheel for the first couple of hours, glancing at the green glowing screen of the radar.

Usually the radar screen was blank, but every now and then a dot would appear, indicating another fishing boat, a tanker, or a freighter. Because the work was monotonous, shifts at the wheel were short. With the motion of the long swells of the open ocean and the droning of the *Fair Wind*'s 265-horsepower diesel engine, it was easy to get lulled to sleep.

Occasionally Dave raised a different fishing vessel on the radio, both to keep himself alert and to check on the other boat's progress. On this trip, the nearest vessel was the *Sea Fever*, a commercial lobster boat also heading to Georges Bank for a season-ending trip. The two vessels floated five miles apart. Because they had worked in close proximity all summer, the crews were familiar with each other and glad to have a friendly boat nearby should any trouble arise. Both crews had a healthy respect for the ocean and knew that an unforeseen accident could pay a visit at any moment.

Chapter 3

THE FORECAST

ON FRIDAY AFTERNOON ERNIE TOOK HIS TURN AT the wheel. He was swept up by the sense of freedom and contentment he always felt when piloting the *Fair Wind* southeast toward the vast open space of the fishing grounds. Visibility was good, and the *Fair Wind* easily rose up and over the gentle five-foot swells. Its bow smoothly parted the seas at the front of the vessel, a white wake trailing astern.

With the sun low in the southwestern sky behind him, Ernie looked out over the platinum sea and felt that he was exactly where he should be, at the right place and the right time. The seemingly boundless world of the North Atlantic was just where he belonged at this stage in his life. He was healthy, single, and happy, with the personal freedom to do whatever he wanted with his young life.

At 4:00 p.m. Rob Thayer took the wheel as the *Fair Wind* passed through an area known as the Great Round Shoal, putting the island of Nantucket behind its stern. Rob paid close attention to the radar screen, as he would soon be crossing the shipping lanes to and from Boston Harbor.

Crossing the lanes could be dangerous because of the amount of traffic that used them. A small boat like the *Fair Wind* wouldn't stand a chance in a collision with a much larger oil tanker or a freighter, and many of the fishing vessels that have simply disappeared probably met their ends this way.

Often the crew of a massive ship doesn't even realize that they've run over a smaller vessel, or worse, the ship's skipper pretends not to notice and continues onward. The only clue that later links the ship to the accident is a streak of paint from the smaller boat running along the ship's hull. (A ship's radar may not pick up a small boat at all, and even if it does, it's often too late to avoid the collision.)

On this evening the *Fair Wind* crossed the shipping lanes without incident and continued east toward

Georges Bank. The *Fair Wind* would be one of only a handful of boats working an area larger than southern New England—all the more reason for the *Fair Wind* to maintain radio communication with the *Sea Fever*, also heading out for lobster.

As Rob steered the boat, he periodically checked the radio for weather forecasts, and the reports continued to call for fair conditions. These reports were announced on a fixed schedule every six hours, with the next report due at 11:00 p.m.

While Rob manned the helm, Billy stayed below deck with the others sleeping or reading. Once on the Bank, Billy would be as busy as the rest of the crew, although he'd be at the wheel much of the time while Ernie, Rob, and Dave worked on deck retrieving traps dropped a week earlier.

Because this was their last trip of the season, they'd be spending considerable time stacking traps and coiling line once the gear was hauled up and the lobsters were dropped in the saltwater tanks under the back deck. Little motion would be wasted, as each man knew exactly what was expected of him. By this time in the season they could anticipate their fellow crewmates' each and every movement.

By working as a group they would push one another to labor far harder than if they were toiling alone. After the second or third day, the grueling effort would catch up with their endurance. Lifting gear, which one man might have done alone on the first day, may now require assistance, and the crew would increasingly depend on one another. This would also be the time crewmen needed to be a bit more deliberate to avoid slipping on deck or getting a leg or an arm caught in a line.

It's an unwritten rule that the whole crew remains on deck until the job at hand is completed. If a crewman on deck got hurt or caught in a dangerous situation, his very life might depend on immediate assistance. Without help, a man entangled in a trapline could be yanked overboard in the blink of an eye. It would be a long way down to a watery grave before his crewmates even noticed he was missing.

Now, however, the heavy work was still twelve hours away, and the crew was relaxed and rested. Billy Garnos took over for Rob on the wheel, and Rob went below and settled into his bunk as the *Fair Wind* cut through the seas on its southeastward course.

As the *Fair Wind* approached the halfway mark

to Billy Garnos's preferred fishing grounds on the southeastern edge of Georges Bank, a sinister force was collecting itself to the south. A low-pressure system was taking shape, silently gathering strength off the South Carolina coast. The weather service knew about this low-pressure system and predicted a northeastward trajectory that would take the storm toward Nova Scotia, well east of Georges Bank. The only effect of the storm forecast for Georges Bank was for a few showers and windy conditions on Saturday. But the storm had other plans.

Forecasting weather at sea in 1980 was more challenging than it is today and far more difficult than forecasting land-based weather. A land storm passes over several dozen monitoring stations manned by meteorologists with the latest technology, making it virtually impossible to surprise a region. An ocean storm, on the other hand, has far fewer monitors. A meteorologist must rely on satellite images, high-altitude atmosphere balloons, weather buoys, and reports from passing ships. Two of these four monitoring tools were not available on that November night. Not only were two weather buoys broken, but no ships had crossed directly through the low-pressure system's path. At the time, the third tool, satellite imagery, was not reliable, still unable to clearly penetrate the high atmospheric cloud cover.

The meteorologist in charge of the National Weather Service office in Boston, Rodney Winslow, was not comfortable predicting ocean weather with limited information. He had repeatedly warned his superiors about the broken buoy at Georges Bank, writing in one memo: "This buoy is extremely important to us in New England. It serves as one of the few reliable observation points in an area where a tremendous number of fishing vessels operate daily....I urge every effort be made to bring and maintain these buoys on continuous operational status. Must we once again open ourselves to political repercussion because of the failure of an important piece of equipment?"

The weather buoy in question had begun to malfunction as early as the spring of 1980, when it simply stopped reporting. In early August, it was hit by a ship, causing further damage. At-sea repairs were made on August 11, but on September 6 the wind sensor failed. Winslow's request to have it repaired again was denied by managers at the National Oceanographic and Atmospheric Administration, which oversees both the National Weather Service and the marine weather buoys. NOAA was wrestling with budget limitations and decided to wait to repair the buoy until January, when a new, improved type of wind sensor would be ready to install.

Of course, Ernie, Billy, Rob, and Dave knew nothing about this. So far the trip out to the Bank had been smooth going, and when Billy listened to the 11:00 p.m. weather forecast, he heard nothing new.

The *Fair Wind* steamed eastward, as long, gentle swells rolled beneath its hull.

Chapter 4

IN THE MONSTER'S GRIP

ERNIE WOKE FROM HIS SLEEP AT 6:00 A.M. AND KNEW immediately that something was wrong. The *Fair Wind* pitched violently, and he could feel the boat shudder with each breaking wave. As he threw on a pair of pants and slid into his work boots, he wondered what had happened to the predicted five-to-ten-foot seas. In the wheelhouse he found Dave on the wheel and Billy and Rob standing beside him. Outside, clouds of white spray slammed the windshield as the *Fair Wind* lurched through heavy swells.

"Can you believe this?" Billy said to Ernie.

Ernie glanced out the wheelhouse windows and saw a twenty-foot wave advancing toward them. "It sure doesn't look like five-to-ten-foot seas," said Ernie sarcastically. "What did the five a.m. report say?"

"The forecast changed," Billy said. "It called for a gale warning with winds of thirty to forty knots and seas eight to fourteen feet. Dave was on the wheel, and he woke me when he heard that. When I got up here, the wind was already pushing fifty knots, and the seas were easily running fifteen to twenty feet. And it's getting worse by the minute."

The crew knew they were too far out to sea to do anything other than keep the *Fair Wind*'s bow pointed into the seas, maintain position, and take the beating. They wanted to avoid waves breaking on the stern at the rear, which could damage gear and bury the boat under tons of churning water. If the weather forecast was even remotely credible, they were now facing the worst that the storm had to give, and things would soon improve.

Outside, the wind roared and rain flew almost horizontally, the drops splattering the boat like shotgun pellets. Visibility shrank to just twenty-five to fifty feet, and a low cloud cover hovered just above the ocean. The angry, breaking seas filled the air with frothing foam, making it difficult to determine where the sea ended and the sky began. The crew would haul no traps today, but they hoped that if the storm quickly subsided, they might be able to work on Sunday.

Billy had Dave position the boat so that it was headed directly into the wind with the waves striking a couple of degrees to port, which was the side of the pilothouse made of welded steel. The doors to the pilothouse were on the starboard side, and Billy didn't want them to take a beating.

Billy wasn't worried about the weather as much as he was angry about the forecast. Just seven hours earlier, the 11:00 p.m. forecast had called for favorable weather. Had he known the day before that a storm would hit the Bank today, he would have turned back and waited for the weather to clear. Now it was too late.

Billy raised the *Sea Fever* on the radio to see how it was making out. The captain of the *Sea Fever*, Peter Brown, had taken the same action as Billy, pointing the bow into the sea, waiting it out. Brown made it clear that he too was fuming mad that the weather forecast had been dead wrong. By the time the 5:00 a.m. forecast predicted a gale, his boat was already in its grip. He wondered how the weather service could have made such a dire mistake.

By 7:00 a.m. the seas had grown to twenty-five feet, and some barrels of bait had come loose on the *Fair Wind*'s deck, rolling from side to side and banging the rail. The barrels could damage the boat or be swept overboard, where a loose line could become tangled in the propeller. If a propeller stops spinning, a boat can no longer be steered, and in high seas the results can be fatal. Without propeller power, the boat will soon be sideways, or "abeam," to the waves, and rough seas can quickly roll the boat.

Ernie and Billy had no choice but to risk going on deck to secure the barrels in spite of the danger. At any moment an ill-timed breaking wave might sweep them overboard. When they left the safety of the pilothouse, the force of the wind staggered them as if they'd been punched by an unseen fist.

The wind was so strong that it tore the tops off the waves. Yellow spindrift, ocean spray with the consistency of shaving cream, raced through the air, blurring and stinging their eyes. The two men found it difficult to breathe, so thick was the air with foam and water. The cold rain pelted them like tiny stones stinging their skin as the two fought to keep their balance on the heaving deck. The wind roared in their ears. Beyond the boat's railing there was an absence of color: all that was visible was the white-and-gray churning sea.

Fighting their way toward the stern, Ernie and Billy had the disconcerting view of the seas converging on the boat. They faced the stern, and when the *Fair Wind* climbed up a wave, they were looking down into the area between waves called the trough, then as the boat crested the wave, they were looking up, hearing the whine of the propeller, wondering if it was grabbing water or just whirling around in the foam.

Ernie and Billy worked hunched over and low to the deck, wrestling with the barrels being buffeted by the forty-three-knot gusts. Slowly, working together, they shoved the barrels back into position and lashed them down. Then they began securing the other equipment, desperate to get all the work done now so they wouldn't have to come back out later.

At 8:00 a.m. Ernie took over the wheel, and an exhausted Dave Berry retreated below to try to get some rest. The seas had grown to thirty feet. Ernie had to give more engine power to maintain headway up and over the waves. The *Fair Wind* responded, but occasionally part of a wave crashed on its bow before the vessel asserted itself.

Neither Ernie nor Billy, who had ten years' experience fishing on the Bank, had ever seen waves build so rapidly. It seemed that each advancing wave was a bit bigger than the last.

By 9:00 a.m. the seas were thirty-five to forty feet, and the wind had increased yet again, to sustained speeds of fifty to sixty knots. Every now and then a gust would roar in at seventy knots, and those savage blasts seemed to probe the boat for weaknesses. Each time a particularly vicious wave slammed the bow, Ernie felt thankful the *Fair Wind*'s hull was made of steel. He kept telling himself it couldn't get any worse.

The height of the waves began to equal the length of the boat. Ernie steered and powered the *Fair Wind* more by feel than sight, and he did his best to keep the boat's bow facing into the oncoming waves to reduce the incredible pounding blows they hurled at him.

Chapter 5

PITCHPOLED

THE CREW OF THE *FAIR WIND* LOOKED OUT AT SEAS that only a handful of people on earth have ever seen. It was now 11:00 a.m., and the waves had climbed to an unimaginable sixty to seventy feet of cresting fury.

The boat's location, right on the edge of the continental shelf on Georges Bank, was the very worst place to be. As the waves came off the deep water of the Atlantic and hit shallower waters on the shelf, they grew steeper, and the steeper the wave, the more likely it is to break upon itself and whatever else lies in its path. The waves were so enormous that they literally could not support themselves. The tops broke free of the main body of the wave and plunged straight downward, like an avalanche falling off a cliff. The wind, spiking at seventy-eight knots, added its blows to the giant waves by tearing off what was left of the wave top and flinging it through the air horizontally.

Despite the terrific beating, the men of the *Fair Wind* had faith in their boat. There was no sense of panic, just a sense of awe at the power of the storm and an impatience for it to move on. The sturdy little boat continued to meet every monstrous wave, and with a little help from Ernie on the throttle, it climbed up, up, up, ever higher until its bow was out of the water at the top of the wave. There was a split-second pause as the vessel hung on the crest of each wave with its propellers out of the water, spinning wildly and uselessly in the air and foam. Then, with the bow pointed downward, Ernie backed off the throttle and down the boat went, hitting the trough in a spray of water that shot upward like a geyser. Clenching the wheel, Ernie saw the next wave coming and gave the engine more diesel, as he positioned the bow yet again to take the wave head-on.

Ernie may not have noticed it, but over the last couple of hours the interval between each wave had gotten shorter, allowing less and less time to recover from each punch. The crew felt like boxers in a ring, the ocean a quick, relentless opponent. They assumed they were suffering the storm's strongest punches, but in reality these waves were only jabs. The storm was still holding back.

Much of the time all Ernie could see out the windshield was foam and spray, but he had a sense of the spacing and timing between the waves, and he did his best to get ready for the next one. The vessel was doing almost everything Ernie asked of it, and with Billy's instructions, the crew felt they could weather this monster.

No serious thought was given to donning survival suits because the men, while concerned and exhausted, didn't feel any impending doom. Nor did they want to be encumbered by the suits, which made movement slow. The suit's mitten-like hand coverings would make it difficult to pilot the boat or perform other tasks that had to be done in a split second.

Billy called the *Sea Fever* again, and this time the radio static made it difficult to hear Peter Brown. But at least he knew the vessel was still afloat when Peter's garbled voice responded. Billy also heard from another fishing boat, the *Broadbill*. He wouldn't wish this storm on even his worst enemy, but it was comforting to know he wasn't facing it alone. While it would be extremely difficult to maneuver to a boat in distress, Billy knew that all three boats would give it a try in an emergency.

Billy had been through the stress of combat in Vietnam, and what was now happening on Georges Bank had a similar feel. His senses were in overdrive, and he felt wary, particularly because his enemy—the unrelenting waves—was impossible to predict. Sometimes they hit the boat from a slightly different angle; sometimes they came packed tightly together; and sometimes the waves varied in size.

For six hours, Billy had been watching the huge dark walls of water advance toward the *Fair Wind*, and just when he thought they were due for a lull, more enormous waves rose out of the gloom. He wasn't saying much to the crew simply because there was nothing to say and nothing more they could do. They just had to stay sharp, be ready to react, and ride it out.

Ernie had been manning the wheel since 8:00 a.m., so Billy decided to take the next shift around 11:30. The wind, unbelievably, was not abating, but still increasing in speed, now hitting an incredible eighty-seven knots. Billy took the wheel while in a trough, and Ernie stood beside him to port. On the opposite side of Billy, Rob Thayer stood ready to do whatever the skipper asked of him. Dave Berry was still in his bunk below.

Peering out the windshield, Ernie's face went pale, and his eyes widened as the tallest wave yet, a wall of water as big as a ten-story building, close to one hundred feet tall, roared toward the *Fair Wind*. Billy held steady on the wheel and pushed the throttle for more power, and the boat started to climb the vertical slope. None of the three men said a word, but all three must have been thinking the same thing, hoping to coax the *Fair Wind* forward. *Come on, come on. Climb!*

As the vessel reached the halfway point up the wave, it seemed the propellers stopped biting because of all the foam, and Billy strained forward, willing his boat to climb still higher.

For a half second, the boat hung on the face of the wave. Then the men, wide-eyed with terror, watched the curling summit of the wave top collapse on them. There was no time to shout, only a split second to brace themselves, as tons of churning water crashed directly onto the *Fair Wind*.

The impact, sounding like an explosion, spun the vessel 180 degrees like a toy. Anything not bolted down went flying, and the three men in the pilothouse struggled to remain standing and avoid getting slammed into the walls or windshields. Dave Berry, still below, was likely hurled out of his bunk and into the air before crashing into the bunks opposite his.

In those agonizing slow-motion seconds, Ernie felt a sickening sensation as the *Fair Wind* careened wildly down the very wave it had tried to climb. The boat was in free fall, accelerating from the force of the wave on its stern. Its nose smacked into the trough below, striking the ocean with incredible force. The bow bored into the sea, and Ernie felt the stern of the vessel, propelled by the avalanching wave behind the boat, go whipping up and over the submerged bow. Ernie smashed into the pilothouse ceiling, which was now below him. The *Fair Wind* had "pitchpoled," flipped end over end, and was now upside down.

Thousands of gallons of frigid water poured into the wheelhouse, seizing the men in a swirling embrace. In only a second or two, the upside-down wheelhouse had almost completely filled with green seawater. Stunned, Ernie was tossed about as if in a washing machine. It was wet, cold, and dark, but he instinctively pushed upward and hit his head on the wheelhouse floor, where four or five inches of air had become trapped. Although he was totally disoriented, uncertain if he was upside down or right side up, his brain still screamed, *Get out, get out!*

Ernie took what air he could and ducked his head into the water to try to figure out where he was. Below, he saw a faint patch of light. Deciding to swim for it, Ernie dove but hit his head on what may have been the windshield. He turned to go back for more air. But the air pocket had vanished.

Ernie thought to himself, *It's all over. So this is how it happens. I'll be dead in a couple of minutes.* Amazingly, he did not panic, nor shrink from confronting his death. He simply thought, *If it's going to happen, it happens.*

The survival instinct, however, is strong, and Ernie was not about to help the ocean do its dirty work. He still had one option left—besides giving up—and that was to go back down and swim toward the light.

Operating on adrenaline, he dove yet again, hoping the faint patch of light was an opening and not just a windshield. With lungs screaming for air, he slipped through a small hole. As soon as he felt his legs free of the boat, he looked in the direction he thought was the surface and stroked and kicked with all his strength. He couldn't hold his breath much longer. Ernie clawed his way through the water, knowing that if he didn't surface in a second or two, he would lose consciousness.

The upward climb seemed an eternity, but just before Ernie felt he would either breathe in the ocean or black out, his head cleared the surface. As he gasped for air, a wave washed over him. He kicked furiously to raise his head a bit higher. Even when his head was above the wave, breathing was difficult because of the foam in the air. He was taking both air and water into his lungs.

Ernie saw the hull of the *Fair Wind*, and for a second this sight seemed so surreal, so strange, that his mind could not grasp what had happened. Amazingly, the boat's propeller still whirled at full speed, but Ernie couldn't hear the whine of the propeller over the howling wind and crashing seas. He had emerged on the windward side of the vessel, and he tried to grip the overturned hull. It was impossible, however, to secure a handhold on the smooth, slick metal.

Although Ernie tried to stay with the vessel, the wind drove the boat away faster than he could swim. He experienced a sense of deep dread; his only hope for survival was drifting along with the boat.

All manner of debris, from lines to smashed pieces of wood, was swirling around as Ernie fought to stay with the boat, but with each passing second the *Fair Wind* was pushed farther away. Just staying afloat became a struggle for Ernie with his boots and jacket weighing him down. Fortunately, his boots were untied and he kicked them free, and then he squirmed out of his jacket.

Exhausted, and barely able to move his arms, Ernie spotted a bucket floating nearby and grabbed it; he turned it over to trap some air inside and used it as a float. The full magnitude of what had happened now hit him like a blow to the stomach. The situation looked hopeless, and already the cold November seas of 55 degrees were sucking the warmth out of his body and sapping what little strength he had left.

In a strange way, however, in those first few moments after capsizing, Ernie had already been lucky several times. First, he had stayed conscious, despite being thrown about in the pilothouse. Second, the fact that he did not have a survival suit on saved his life: its buoyancy would have prevented him from swimming downward toward the opening in the pilothouse. And, when he did surface, it was away from the slicing propeller. He also had the good fortune to have his boots untied or he would have surely sunk under their weight. And finally, the bucket had floated within reach as if guided there by the very wind and waves that had pitchpoled the *Fair Wind*.

Yes, a few small strokes of luck fell Ernie's way, but now, with the boat drifting away and Ernie fighting to stay afloat in the unrelenting seas, he was going to need more than luck to survive; he'd need a miracle.

Chapter 6

DECISIONS

So far, in a hungry sea that afforded no second chances, Ernie had made all the right decisions. But now he had an agonizing choice: continue clinging to the plastic bucket for buoyancy or risk letting it go and trying to somehow claw his way back to the *Fair Wind*. If he did not make it to the boat, he knew he would be lost in the abyss of unforgiving seas. He'd be dead within an hour.

Panting with exhaustion, and dressed only in socks, jeans, and a sweatshirt, Ernie tightly hugged the bucket, his only ally against the storm. In many ways, Ernie's predicament mirrored that of the fishermen who had plied these waters more than a century earlier. Those men left their schooners in small dories to haul in their catch, and if the weather turned against them, they couldn't always make it back to the mother ship. Many died after the wind and waves separated them from their schooners when snow, rain, darkness, or fog closed in like a curtain, eliminating visibility and any hope of finding the ship.

Ernie tried to gather his wits and consider his next move, but it was difficult to think clearly in that violent world of waves and wind. When the sea wasn't crashing on top of him, the salty spray came hurtling across its surface, stinging his face and eyes and smacking his head like buckshot.

The mental strain was tremendous. In the span of a few minutes he had gone from riding out the storm in the pilothouse to facing what he thought was certain death when the *Fair Wind* pitchpoled. And now he was fighting to stay afloat in the open ocean. Overwhelmed, Ernie needed time to collect his thoughts, but the sea, cold and impersonal, refused to let him rest. The *Fair Wind* was more than fifty feet away and quickly drifting farther.

Intuitively, Ernie knew that the temporary comfort of the bucket was just that, temporary. His only hope for survival was to get back to the boat and stay with it. For some of us, this might have been the moment when we hung our heads and gave up, or denied the reality of the situation and stayed with the bucket. Somehow, however, Ernie resisted the temptation to do either.

Reluctantly and with a sense of trepidation, Ernie let the bucket go and faced the void alone. With what little strength he had left he started swimming toward the *Fair Wind*. The same waves that pushed the boat away were now helping Ernie along. He found that if he timed his kicking just right, he could actually bodysurf down the face of a wave by stretching his arms out directly in front of him.

When each house-sized wave broke on him, he struggled back to the surface. Then he swam again until he felt the next wave propel him forward, bodysurfing as best he could toward the overturned hull. The hull came in and out of view, disappearing when Ernie was in a trough but reappearing whenever he was lifted by a wave.

After riding five or six waves he reached the *Fair Wind*, but as before, he found it impossible to climb on top of the slimy hull. Surrounded by foam and shrieking wind, Ernie found it difficult to tell if the propeller was still turning. He decided to avoid the stern and the potentially deadly slicing of the propeller. Instead he turned toward the bow.

As he kicked and stroked, he could feel his power diminish with each move and realized he had only a few more minutes of strength left before he would no longer be able to keep his head above the foam. Each time a wave buried him, he fought to the surface for a quick breath of precious oxygen before the next one came. His heart pounded so hard it felt like it might explode.

Because he was in the water and not on the hull, he was losing body heat approximately twenty-four times faster than he would in air of the same temperature. He had been immersed in the ocean for half an hour, and his dexterity was starting to suffer along with his energy.

The immense size of the waves did not help Ernie's chances. The higher the waves, the more energy a survivor spends just trying to keep his head above water. The expended effort only adds to the speed of the chilling hypothermia moving inward from the body's extremities. It is known that waves over twenty feet hurt survival chances significantly, and Ernie was locked in hand-to-hand combat with waves three times that size. If he did not get out of the water soon, all of his luck and good decisions would be wasted, serving only to postpone the inevitable.

As he rounded the bow, he saw an incredible sight on the other side of the hull: a rubber life raft, fully inflated. It was a bright orange, round, dome-canopied raft, approximately six feet in diameter, tethered by a long line to the *Fair Wind*. Ernie's heart soared. Not only did he see an opportunity to escape the bone-chilling water, but hope returned that the other crewmen had gotten out of the boat and were inside the raft. He swam toward the raft, careful to keep out of the way of the drifting *Fair Wind*, which threatened to overtake him.

The six-man Givens life raft looked like a small tent resting atop two large doughnut-shaped tubes. A fabric floor stretched across its bottom, and inflatable ribs led to the top, where a tiny beacon was mounted. For stability, a large ballast bag hung on the bottom underwater. It was designed to flood with 2,900 pounds of water, and this weight would hold the raft upright in heavy seas and prevent it from flipping over and tumbling across the ocean's surface.

The raft had been mounted atop the pilothouse. It had been in a container designed, should the vessel capsize, to float free of the boat and then self-inflate from CO_2 cartridges inside. Fortunately, the tether from the raft down to the boat had been long enough for the raft to reach the surface. Had that tether been just five feet shorter, the raft would not have reached the surface and instead would have been torn from the line by the seas and blown away.

When Ernie reached the raft, he managed to use the small boarding ladder to heave himself up and crawl inside. No one was there. He collapsed on the floor of the raft and held back a cry of anguish.

Although Ernie was finally out of the sea, the waves still pummeled him, crashing atop the raft and crushing him into the fabric floor. Yet he was spared their full force because the raft was floating on the lee side (or downwind of the wind and waves) of the hull, which partially protected him from the towering walls of water. Four or five inches of water sloshed around the bottom, so he tried to find a sitting position with his back against the dome to keep some of his body out of the water.

The raft itself was being jerked violently on its tether, and Ernie feared the line might tear the raft's fabric at the point where it was secured. But he would not set the raft free. *My friends are down there*, he thought. He still held out hope that maybe, just maybe, one of them would emerge from the boat, and he'd be able to haul him in. Perhaps, he thought, they were already free of the boat, and he simply couldn't see them in the churning water and foam. Billy Garnos, Rob Thayer, and Dave Berry—one or all of them might make it, he told himself. But deep inside he knew the odds were incredibly low. Still, he held his silent vigil alongside the overturned *Fair Wind* and refused to release the raft from its line.

Icy water poured into the raft, and the curtained doorway did little to stop the flood. The tether was tied to the raft directly in front of the raft's entrance hole, which meant the opening faced into the wind and oncoming seas. The walls of the raft could not muffle the roaring and hissing of the waves.

Every now and then Ernie stuck his head out of the raft's opening to look for another survivor, but all he could see was the ocean washing over the *Fair*

Wind's hull. There was no horizon, no sky, just moving hills of gray and green. He was shivering now, and his soggy sweatshirt seemed to make him feel colder, but he knew any material around his skin was better than none. His sweatshirt, jeans, and socks added a slight degree of warmth because they trapped a bit of water warmed by his body.

Ernie looked up and saw a small bag hanging on the wall of the canopy and reached up and snagged it. Inside was a small plastic tag of instructions about the raft. With the raft pitching wildly it was difficult to read, but Ernie managed to decipher the first of several instructions, which said to free the raft from the tether as soon as possible. A minute later a wave slammed into the raft and, as he fell forward, the instruction tag came loose and went out with the cascading water.

Ernie brought himself back to a sitting position. He poked his head out of the raft, looking at the bowline knot that secured the line to the raft, now knowing he should release the knot immediately. He had been inside the raft for roughly thirty minutes. He looked at the *Fair Wind*'s hull and decided that until it settled farther down in the water he would not release the raft. He simply could not leave as long as even a shred of hope remained that his friends were alive. What he didn't know was that the constant tugging of the raft on the line was doing damage to the ballast bag beneath him.

FAIR WIND

Chapter 7

THE *SEA FEVER*

APPROXIMATELY TEN MILES NORTH OF WHERE ERNIE was struggling to stay alive, the ferocious storm was battering another boat, the *Sea Fever*. The *Sea Fever* was similar in size and shape to the *Fair Wind*, but this forty-seven-foot lobster boat was made of wood rather than steel. Both its hull and superstructure were painted white, and the front of the pilothouse had four windows made of heavy safety glass, each approximately eighteen inches wide and twelve inches tall.

There was a window and a plywood wall on the port side of the *Sea Fever*, and a window and a two-panel door made of three-quarter-inch plywood on the starboard side. Clear plastic strips formed a curtain at the rear of the pilothouse, allowing quick access to the work deck. Below were the engine compartment, galley, and four bunks outfitted with seat belts so that sleeping crewmen would not be tossed out of bed if the seas kicked up.

The *Sea Fever* was owned by Bob Brown, who later purchased the *Andrea Gail*, whose demise was chronicled in Sebastian Junger's *The Perfect Storm*. Brown had the *Sea Fever* built exactly to his specifications in 1970, and it was his first offshore boat. A few years later, he purchased a second lobster boat, the seventy-foot *Sea Star*. On Saturday, November 22, 1980, both boats were ambushed on Georges Bank by the sudden storm that capsized the *Fair Wind*. Bob was captaining the *Sea Star*; his twenty-three-year-old son, Peter, was captaining the *Sea Fever*.

Peter, who was six feet tall with blue eyes, brown hair, and an easy smile, had a demeanor almost opposite that of his unyielding father. While his hard-driving father pushed his crew to the limit of their endurance and even jeopardized their safety, Peter put his crew's well-being first. He understood that a crew could get just as much accomplished in a more relaxed atmosphere where each individual felt he was part of a team. Peter even encouraged suggestions from the crew, whereas Bob typically glared at the crewman who offered a suggestion, then told him to get back to work. Consequently, the men who worked for both the Browns wrangled for future trips with Peter rather than Bob. Peter was more than happy to captain the *Sea Fever* to get out from under the critical eye of his father.

On the Saturday of the storm, Peter's crew included three young men, all of whom had been working on the *Sea Fever* since the start of the season. Gary Brown (no relation to Bob or Peter) was the oldest of the group at age twenty-seven and was the only married crew member. His wife, Honour, was pregnant with their first child. Gary, who loved to fish even for recreation, was already talking about how someday he would own his own boat and teach his son or daughter all about commercial fishing. From the moment Honour first met Gary, she knew fishing was his life, and she accepted that. Living in Plymouth, Massachusetts, afforded Gary plenty of opportunities to fish, and friends were amazed that even after working on the *Sea Fever* for five straight days, he'd spend his day off back on the water surf casting for stripers or paddling a canoe on a pond in search of trout.

Gary and Honour had a strong marriage, and they often celebrated his return from Georges Bank by going out with friends for Chinese food and then taking in a movie. Sometimes Gary would surprise his wife by bringing home lobster, scallops, or swordfish and preparing a great meal for just the two of them. Gary did this in spite of Bob Brown's policy of not allowing any of the crew to take home the catch.

The year before he worked for Peter, Gary was working on the *Sea Star* for Bob, and he decided to smuggle two large lobsters off the boat. As the boat was nearing its home port, Gary secretly took the lobsters out of the tank and put them in his duffel bag. As the crew prepared to leave the boat under Bob Brown's watchful eye, Gary's duffel bag, which lay on the deck, started to move. Fellow crewman Richard Rowell whispered and motioned to Gary that his bag was "walking." Gary quickly picked up the bag, slung it over his shoulder, and walked by Bob Brown, wishing him a nice weekend. Bob was none the wiser, and that night Gary and Honour enjoyed another of Gary's great seafood dinners.

Friends of Gary knew him as a handsome, feisty Irishman with red hair and freckles. He was five feet, eleven inches tall with a barrel chest and built like a rock. Peter thought of Gary as the perfect crewmate because he'd never let anyone outwork him. He had a great sense of humor and almost always had a big smile on his face. Peter recognized that besides Gary's strong work ethic, he was reliable and quite handy, and he made him the deck boss of the *Sea Fever*.

The other two crew members, Richard Rowell and Brad Bowen, loved working on the *Sea Fever*, in large part because of their good-natured captain and deck boss. Rowell, at age twenty-three, was the older of the two and had been in the marines, rising to the rank of sergeant. When his hitch in the service was up he returned to his hometown of Danvers, Massachusetts, and looked for work.

The first job Richard took was at a machine shop, but like Ernie Hazard he found working indoors stifling. His coworkers didn't appreciate how Rowell propped open the doors to the shop in the dead of winter to let in the fresh air. A friend suggested Rowell join him in commercial fishing, saying, "If you want to make money, get on one of Bob Brown's boats." But when Rowell tracked down Brown and asked for a job, Brown took a cold look at Rowell's five-foot, six-inch frame and said, "Forget it, you're too small to handle the work on my boats." Rowell didn't argue, didn't tell him about his service in the marines, but instead simply said, "Just give me a chance."

Bob Brown may have been difficult to work for, but he was fair. If someone asked for a chance, Bob was likely to grant one, and then watch him crumble after a few days of working around the clock at sea. Bob was tough as nails, and he expected his crew members to be the same, or they didn't last more than a trip or two.

Brown was also short in stature, and as he sized up Rowell, he might have seen something of himself in the young greenhorn. Sheer muscle and size weren't the only factors for work on a boat—stamina was equally important. More than once Brown had outworked larger, stronger men, leaving them gasping like fish that had just been gaffed while he continued to haul gear as if he was just getting started.

"Be ready to go in a couple days," Brown said to Rowell. On that first trip, Rowell had to endure the demands of Bob Brown, who treated new crew like workhorses. This was likely Brown's way of quickly weeding out the slackers, and Rowell wasn't going to give Brown anything to complain about. He was a dynamo on deck, and although Brown never once gave him a compliment, Rowell knew he had cemented a position as a permanent crewman when Brown started calling him Sarge after he learned of Rowell's military experience. The nickname stuck.

As Sarge learned the business, he heard how other owners were far more flexible with their crews. But he also knew that when you fished on a boat owned by Bob Brown, you almost always made good money. The money Sarge made was not paid to him after each trip as it was on most other lobster boats. Instead, Brown would give the crew a small weekly check, and the majority of what each man made wasn't paid until the end of the year. Brown did this to ensure he had a crew when cold weather hit. He had learned that when a crew member left in the late fall it was tough to find a replacement.

During that first year, Sarge also worked on Bob Brown's other boat, the *Sea Fever*. Sarge found that Peter had much of his father's "sea smarts" but without the inflexible edge. While Bob Brown would haul gear in dangerous conditions, Peter knew when to stop for the safety of the crew. Peter once said to Sarge, "The fish will still be there when the seas ease up."

The fourth crewman aboard the *Sea Fever* during the November storm was Brad Bowen. The nineteen-year-old had grown up in Connecticut, where he attended a private school and played hockey, developing into one of the state's top players. But the 6:00 a.m. practices and grueling schedule of games took their toll on Brad. When it came time for college, he had had enough of hockey, and he didn't investigate athletic scholarships. Instead, he decided to pursue his passion for skiing and attended the University of Utah.

The relief from hockey and the enjoyment of skiing were so great that after just one semester of school Brad decided to take some time off so he could ski almost every day and work odd jobs at night. When spring rolled around, he headed back to New England and started looking for work. He had a cousin who was an inshore lobster fisherman in Marblehead, Massachusetts, and Brad asked him about opportunities as a fisherman. Brad got the same advice Sarge received: "If you don't mind working your tail off, contact Bob Brown because his boats make the most money."

Brad met with Bob and within days he was at work mending gear, getting ready for the upcoming season. Brad's initial opinion of Bob Brown was similar to Sarge's. "Bob Brown was almost ruthless the way he drove us," recalls Brad, "and if I did something wrong, he'd sure let me know about it. Giving compliments for good work was just not in his mindset—he expected everything to be done perfectly and quickly."

When the season started, however, luck shined on Brad, and he was assigned to the *Sea Fever*, captained by Peter Brown, with Gary Brown as the deck boss. "Gary was a great teacher," says Brad. "I learned about the boat, the sea, and lobsters all at once. Gary was like a big brother to me, and when I saw he had a tattoo of a lobster on his arm, one of the first things I did when we were back in port was to have the same tattoo put on my arm."

He also learned from Peter and Sarge, and what really stuck in his mind was hearing Sarge say that working on the boat was tougher than the marines. "I loved a challenge, and I took that to heart. I had a sense of satisfaction that I was succeeding at something extremely difficult. And we were paid well for what we did, which is the ultimate incentive."

Brad's initiation in commercial fishing wasn't all smooth sailing, however. Twice the first season he fell overboard when he lost his footing from the momentum of dropping a trap over. Each time when he got back on board, shaken and unnerved, he shouted, "I quit!" But after a few hours he'd change his mind.

The third time Brad went overboard he came within a minute of losing his life. He had just dropped a trap over, and the line to the trap wrapped around his ankle, pulling him off the boat.

Sarge saw what happened and shouted at Brad, "Are you in the lines?" Brad was on the surface and screamed yes. Sarge asked the question because he knew the weight of the trap made it impossible to haul the line back in by hand, so the crew scrambled to get their end of the line through the hauler. Meanwhile, Brad knew that within a second or two the slack in the line was going to be taken up by the sinking trap. He pulled his fourteen-inch Dexter knife from its sheath on his belt, took one big breath, and went down, bending over at the waist so he could reach the rope. On his first try his knife cut through the line, freeing him from a trip to the bottom of the sea.

The crew hauled him on board, and again Brad looked at Peter and spluttered, "I quit." Once Peter determined Brad was okay, he said, "You can't quit— you just tied the boat record for the number of times one crewman has gone overboard! If you stick around, you'll have the record all to yourself!"

Brad didn't quit and he stayed on as the fourth crew member of the *Sea Fever* for the 1980 season. He thought he'd seen the worst his newfound profession could throw at him. But the November storm would terrify him in an entirely new and agonizingly slow way.

Chapter 8

BLOWOUT

LIKE THE *FAIR WIND*, THE *SEA FEVER* ARRIVED ON Georges Bank early Saturday morning, and the crew hoped to begin working at daylight. Peter Brown awoke at 3:00 a.m. and noticed the boat was riding more roughly than it had been at midnight but not enough to cause alarm, so he went back to sleep. By 4:30 a.m., however, the motion of the boat was so violent that he woke up with a start. He immediately climbed the stairs to the pilothouse. Gary Brown was on the wheel. Gary looked at Peter, shook his head, and muttered, "So much for good weather."

It was still dark, but judging from the pitching of the boat, Peter estimated that the waves were fifteen to twenty feet. Outside, the wind howled, and the plastic strips in the back of the pilothouse snapped every which way. Rain fell in torrents, splattering the boat and adding to the din of the wind and waves.

"We obviously aren't going to be doing any fishing for a while," said Peter. "Why don't you get Brad and Sarge up. I'll move us into fifty fathoms." He took the helm from Gary and turned the boat northwest and into the wind. Should the weather get worse, Peter did not want to get caught where they were: between Munson and Powell Canyons at the southeastern edge of Georges Bank. The topography of the ocean floor in this section of Georges Bank is characterized by mountains and valleys and can drop from 360 to 3,600 feet in just a quarter mile. That variation, coupled with the warm eddies from the Gulf Stream, can produce some of the worst upwelling and turbulence of water anywhere. Waves steepen, causing them to crest and break.

Peter steamed northwest to an area with a fairly uniform bottom, fifty to sixty fathoms deep, then just held position with the bow pointed into the seas. Soon the updated 5:00 a.m. forecast came over the radio. Peter shook his head in disgust as he listened to a markedly different report from the last broadcast at 11:00 p.m. This report now included a gale warning and predicted that the seas would grow to between eight and fourteen feet. *Not only is the forecast late and of no value*, thought Peter, *but it's underestimating the conditions we're already in.*

Peter picked up the radio microphone and called another lobster boat riding out the storm nearby: "*Sea Fever* calling *Broadbill*." Captain Grant Moore of the *Broadbill* answered, and each gave their positions. "We're just jogging along," said Peter, "and got her headed into the seas, holding position. What's going on with this weather? This is no gale, it's a storm; we've got winds gusting up to sixty" knots. Moore, whose vessel was about fifteen miles west of the *Sea Fever*, had no more answers than Peter did but said he'd check back with him in an hour.

Spray from the waves washed over the pilot-house and down onto the *Sea Fever*'s deck. Several inches of water sloshed around Peter's feet beneath the wheel. The whole crew was now gathered in the pilothouse. Although Sarge and Brad were still relatively new to offshore fishing, they knew enough to be concerned.

"All I had to do was look at Peter's face, and I

could see he was worried," recalls Brad. "I knew he was thinking ahead, trying to make sure we'd be in the best shape we could possibly be in if things got worse. This was the first storm I'd ever been in, so I just waited for instructions. I watched Peter goose the engine to get us up and over the waves and then ease off as we went down their backside. It seemed each hour the waves grew larger, and by midmorning there were some that were forty to fifty feet. No one had to tell me this was trouble; I could see it in their eyes. We all put life jackets on. We probably would have put survival suits on if we could have maneuvered in them. That's how bad it was getting."

The seas had grown so violent that the fifty-pound bait boxes lashed to the deck came loose. They began sliding back and forth in the deck water, sometimes blocking the scuppers that allowed water to drain from the enclosed deck. The water pouring onto the deck was rising, so Gary and Brad went to fix the problem.

On the deck, Brad had to crawl to escape the force of the wind. "I just could not believe the wind—if I stuck my head up past the gunnels it felt like getting slapped. I couldn't hear anything other than the wind roaring in my ears, and there was foam scudding through the air mixed with the rain. I was worried a big wave was going to sweep over the boat and take me with it. Gary and I worked as fast as we could. We grabbed those bait boxes and just hurled them overboard."

At 11:00 a.m. the men heard the updated weather forecast for Georges Bank, which was finally catching up with reality. Still, however, the report was understated: "Storm warning in effect at 10:00 a.m. . . . Northwest winds forty to fifty knots gradually diminishing to twenty to thirty knots overnight and to westerly at twenty to twenty-five knots Sunday. Rain and fog with visibilities one to three miles but locally near zero. East portion ending by late afternoon. Seas fifteen to twenty-five feet rest of today subsiding tonight." This was the first report that mentioned a storm, but the storm had been raging for six hours. The wind and wave predictions would have to be doubled to match what was happening just beyond the windows of the *Sea Fever*.

The advancing waves were the size of two- and three-story homes, and the length of the troughs between each oncoming wave varied. Sarge had never witnessed conditions even remotely like this, and mixed with his apprehension was a feeling of pure awe. The power of both wind and sea was almost beyond human comprehension. His senses were electric. He felt ready to spring into action, but he wasn't sure what that action would be. In the meantime, he braced himself as best he could as the deck heaved and pitched, and he kept a wary eye on each advancing wave.

On the radio, Peter contacted his father, Bob Brown, who was twenty miles to the east on the seventy-foot, steel-hulled *Sea Star*. Through the static Sarge heard Bob Brown say that he too was taking a pounding and that nothing could be done but ride it out.

Bob added that he'd never seen anything like this, and Sarge felt an involuntary shudder go through him. *When Bob Brown says this is unbelievable*, thought Sarge, *we're in trouble*.

Each time the vessel reached the top of a wave, it wildly slid down the backside. When it struck the trough, Sarge steadied himself as spray flew and the boat shook. Sea and foam enveloped the bow, and Sarge held his breath waiting for the *Sea Fever* to reassert itself. As the boat came back up, the process repeated with the vessel climbing the next big wave heading toward them.

The sturdy *Sea Fever* withstood each and every wave until approximately 12:30 p.m. That's when it happened. Peter looked up to see an enormous wave rearing out of the tempest. The wave seemed to be nearly twice the size of the others, and on its top was fifteen feet of breaking white water.

Peter gave the boat more throttle and then watched in horror as the wave hurled its full fury down on the vessel. He then heard an earsplitting *pow!*

The water, as if concrete, hit the windshield, blasting away two of the pilothouse's four panels. Torrents flooded in. Peter had managed to duck as the wave struck. Although the impact staggered him, he somehow remained at the wheel and gave the engine a bit more juice. He hoped to power the vessel up and over the smothering surf before the wave spun them back down, as had happened to the *Fair Wind*.

Without the windows, the ocean's roar was deafening. As soon as the vessel cleared the wave top, Peter turned to his crew to find out if they were alive. Sarge, Gary, and Brad had returned to their feet, stunned, shaken, and wet but uninjured.

"We gotta turn her around!" Peter screamed.

"Do it!" Gary shouted.

If there's one maneuver mariners dread most, it's turning a boat around in huge seas. It's never done unless absolutely necessary, because it exposes the vessel to a broadside hit from a wave. Yet the move was imperative. If Peter kept the *Sea Fever* heading into the seas, the waves would soon send more water through the two shattered window openings. No amount of pumping would be able to keep up with a continual onslaught of seawater pouring through the open panels. Eventually one of several bleak outcomes would result.

The rising water might kill the engine or short the batteries. Or the incoming water could shift the weight so much that the boat could roll in the waves. And finally, even if the boat escaped those fates, it could become so heavy and sluggish that it simply wouldn't be able to climb the next wave. In this case she would broach—slide sideways down the wave— or pitchpole as the *Fair Wind* had done.

There was no time for Peter to choose a particular trough for the turn and no time to talk it over with Gary, the most seasoned of the rest of the crew.

He simply had to make the turn now, before the next wave hit.

As the *Sea Fever* slid down the back of the enormous wave that had smashed the windows, Peter waited until he felt it was in the trough. Then he punched the engine to almost full power and started a tight turn to port. Holding his breath, he took a quick glance out the starboard window. Through the rain he saw the next wave barreling toward the boat like a raging bull, as if it were trying to catch him sideways, beam-on, before the turn was complete. He had maybe eight seconds to make the turn, or the wave would catch the *Sea Fever* in the exposed position and finish it off.

Chapter 9

SWEPT AWAY

ACCORDING TO COAST GUARD MARINE CASUALTY reports, the loss of windshield panels due to breaking seas is the genesis of countless serious accidents and sinkings. Losing the windshield itself may not be the final failure of the boat, but it is often the first thing that goes wrong, leading to a host of complications that even the best of captains cannot overcome.

Peter Brown knew instantly he was facing a critical problem when the windshield panels exploded. His decision to turn the *Sea Fever* and go with following the seas rather than ride head-on into the waves was the right reaction to the emergency. He needed to shelter the bow from the oncoming seas to stop the flow of incoming water, as well as attempt to patch the windows.

As Peter turned the boat, Gary, Sarge, and Brad clung to whatever they could in the pilothouse, knowing that they might get slammed by a wave before the maneuver was complete. They all now understood that they were caught in a life-or-death situation, which might be decided in the next few seconds. No one said a word, and each kept his fears to himself.

Finally, as the *Sea Fever* completed the turn, they collectively exhaled.

The crew's relief was short-lived, however, because a second later a wave caught the boat and hurled it forward. The *Sea Fever* didn't simply ride the giant comber (curling wave) but seemed to fly above it for a hundred feet. A thundering whooshing noise accompanied its flight through the foamy water.

Peter let the breaker pass under the boat and then adjusted his speed to ride on the back of the wave and stay ahead of the next wave's crest. He worked the throttle carefully to keep the *Sea Fever* running at approximately the same speed as the wave. He opened the throttle for a second or two whenever he felt the bow drop and eased off when it lifted too high. Then he turned to Gary and shouted, "Take the wheel! We've got to get these windows patched so we can turn back into it!"

While Sarge and Brad scrambled to bring plywood, hammer, and nails from below, Gary took the wheel, and Peter reached out to the deck and pulled in a coil of nylon rope. The rope was to be his lifeline; Peter had decided that he would be the one to go out on the bow and fix the windows. He felt it was his duty as captain to be the one to take the risk. Sarge would grip the other end of the line, and should Peter go over, they figured they would stand at least a fifty-fifty chance of hauling him back on board.

When the line was secure around Peter's waist, he leaned toward Brad and just inches from his ear shouted, "When I'm out on the bow, pass the hammer and nails through the broken window and then do the same with the plywood."

Brad never had a chance to answer. A wave of approximately seventy feet bore down on the men with a furious rush, breaking just off the stern. The force and the speed of the snarling curler sent the crippled boat careening down its face faster than the propellers could turn.

"I can't control it!" hollered Gary.

In a sickening sideways movement, the *Sea Fever* broached. The boat was caught abeam, or sideways, in the driving onslaught of the sea.

A second later the wave lifted the port side up and drove the starboard side downward. The force knocked the men from their feet and threw them into the air as they heard a terrific *crack!*

The water's impact was so violent that it blew apart most of the starboard side of the pilothouse as if it had been hit by a giant fist. In came the rushing water with a great roar, engulfing all four of the crew. Then, as the boat righted itself, the water rushed out of the pilothouse, sucking Gary and Sarge up from the floor and toward the splintered opening.

The pilothouse was in shambles, littered with shards of wood and glass. Adding to the confusion was the continual blasting buzz of the bilge alarm, signaling that the bottom of the boat had rapidly filled with water. Peter and Brad struggled to their feet and looked through the busted opening. They witnessed a miracle and a nightmare. Sarge was lying up against the rail, the only thing separating him from the ocean, but Gary was out of the boat, floating in the seas with a stunned look on his face.

While Peter took the wheel, Brad helped Sarge up, and the two ran out on the deck. They threw a life ring to Gary, but the wind just whipped it back. A wave crashed over him and he was lost from sight.

"I've lost him!" screamed Brad. "I can't see him!"

"There he is!" shouted Sarge, pointing directly behind the boat. Now the boat was floating thirty feet from Gary. "Don't take your eyes off him!" he shouted to Brad.

Sarge grabbed a line to throw to Gary, but by the time he was ready, Gary had drifted almost fifty feet from the *Sea Fever*. There was no way the line would reach him in the wind. "Hang on, Gary!" he screamed.

Realizing the futility of trying to reach Gary with a rope, Brad started to climb up the rail to dive in.

"No!" shouted Sarge as he grabbed Brad's coat and yanked him back on deck. "Listen to me! Stay in the boat!" Sarge knew that it was going to be difficult to get one man back, and impossible to get two.

Meanwhile, Peter had run down the stairs and into the engine room. Two feet of water sloshed around, but it was not yet high enough to knock out the engine. Peter hurried back up and looked out on deck. Gary was now well behind the boat and drifting off quickly. Peter grabbed the wheel and punched the throttle, taking the risk of turning the boat without trying to time the maneuver.

More water flooded through the broken windshield, but Peter managed to make the turn. He maneuvered the boat within twenty-five feet of Gary, who still floated motionlessly, a dazed expression on his face.

Sarge knew that this was his best chance to reach Gary with the line. This time he waited until the wind would aid him in his throw. He hurled the line out and it fell directly across Gary's shoulder.

Gary made no move to grab the line. He may have been stunned from being hurled through the wall or he may have broken his back.

Sarge and Brad watched in horror as the line slipped off Gary's shoulder. Then another wave carried him out of sight.

"Turn! Turn again!" Sarge shouted to Peter, motioning with his hand.

Once more Peter punched the engine and made the turn. This time around there was no sign of Gary.

Peter stepped from the wheel and shouted through

the back opening of the pilothouse, "Get your survival suits on!"

Brad and Sarge scrambled into the pilothouse just as a wave struck the boat broadside. The wave sent the *Sea Fever* scudding along the breaking face and again driving the starboard side downward.

Peter managed to get to the radio: "Mayday! Mayday! Mayday! This is the *Sea Fever*! We have lost a man overboard! We are just above Powell!"

It was just before 3:00 p.m. when Peter made his distress call. He had given his position north of Powell Canyon, and he knew that Grant Moore on the *Broadbill* and his father in the *Sea Star* were nearby. He also assumed Billy Garnos of the *Fair Wind* remained in the vicinity. Peter waited for an agonizing second, praying that the radio was still working properly in spite of being soaked with water.

Almost immediately Grant responded. "Peter, we're on our way! Keep talking!"

"Gary's gone, we can't find him! The boat is flooding; she might go down any minute! We've got to get off; she won't stay up much longer!"

A new voice broke in on the radio. "Peter, listen to me! Stay with the boat! Your best chance is with the boat!" It was Bob Brown. "We got problems of our own here, and can't make the turn, so just hang on until Grant gets there!"

Grant's voice returned. "Peter, we will be there soon! I've told the Coast Guard what happened! A cutter is on its way, so hang on!"

Grant did not have the heart to tell Peter that it would take a Coast Guard cutter close to twelve hours to reach the scene and that with the hurricane winds a helicopter was out of the question. Grant steered the *Broadbill* into the seas and toward the accident scene.

Part II

Chapter 10

STAY WITH THE BOAT!

Of all the mariners trapped on Georges Bank, Bob Brown was the most experienced. He was forty-three years old, and he'd been fishing since he was fourteen, the year he bought a used skiff from which he caught lobsters along the north shore of Massachusetts. Bob worked his way through larger boats, and at age thirty he began fishing Georges Bank. On the day of the storm he was captaining the seventy-foot *Sea Star* near Corsair Canyon, located approximately twenty miles east-northeast of the *Sea Fever*'s position.

Incredibly, early in the morning when the seas were fifteen to twenty feet, Bob Brown had ordered his crew to haul several traps they had previously dropped. His crew must have wondered if he was homicidal as waves washed over the deck and the pilothouse filled with water three separate times.

One of those crew members was Mike Sosnowski. He was the deck boss of the *Sea Star* and a three-year employee of Bob Brown's. "I was probably the only crew member on the boat that wasn't shocked when Bob had us hauling gear. Once that man got on the fishing grounds, he was there to stay. That was my third year working on the *Sea Star*, and I had become almost numb to the crazy risks Bob took. And that morning was awful. I remember shouting at a crewmate who was just a foot away, but he couldn't hear a thing I said over the roaring of the wind."

Around 8:00 a.m. Bob finally called in the crew, turned the *Sea Star* into the wind, and prepared to ride out the storm. Like the other captains, he couldn't believe the weather forecast could have been so wrong the night before.

Bob was probably the only man on Georges Bank that day who did not feel the cold grip of trepidation. He had survived storms with winds of eighty knots, but even he marveled at how suddenly this storm arose. While his crew considered donning survival suits and some prayed for their safety, Bob Brown took pictures of the waves. He experienced the storm in an almost detached manner, interested in how his boat would perform and eager to learn from the event.

The storm was a formidable challenge to be sure, but not something Bob feared. He simply could not be intimidated by the ocean, even in the face of seventy-foot seas. Bob found the experience fascinating, feeling a sense of pride that his boat was handling seas larger than many mariners believed possible.

Then he heard the Mayday call from Peter. The wonder of watching the storm gave way to anger because he knew he could not immediately go to his son's aid. It was impossible to make any progress going into the teeth of the wind and waves. All he could do was shout to his son on the radio, "Stay with the boat! Your best chance is with the boat!"

———

Fortunately, however, Grant Moore on the *Broadbill* was west of Peter, and he had the waves mostly at his back as he headed toward the foundering *Sea Fever*.

Grant was of lean build with brown hair and intelligent blue eyes. The twenty-five-year-old had a direct manner and a maturity beyond his years. Like the other fishermen, he had Popeye forearms from lifting trap after trap and was not the kind of person you'd pick a fight with. He was friendly with Peter and had tremendous respect for Bob.

Grant's relationship with Bob had started out on the right foot when Bob offered Grant sound advice about lobster fishing on Georges Bank. One day, however, Grant found some of his gear destroyed and he confronted Bob. He suspected Bob had damaged the gear because it was in an area he thought of as his own. Bob told Grant that's exactly what happened and he'd better stay the heck out of that area. Grant responded by saying, "If you ever mess with me again, you'll regret it. Next time talk with me face-to-face."

Surprisingly the two men put this incident behind them, and over the years they developed a friendship and mutual respect. "The reason I had such a good relationship with Bob," says Grant, "is probably because I never had to work for him. Instead we had our own boats. We occasionally even shared information, such as when Bob gave me tips on adding refrigeration to another boat I bought."

The *Broadbill* was a sixty-five-foot steel lobster

boat with a crew of four besides Grant. The crew had hauled gear all day Friday and into the night. Around 1:00 a.m. on Saturday they had to knock off because it started raining so hard they couldn't find the high-flyers (metal flags) marking the traps.

"After we stopped hauling gear," recalls Grant, "one of the crew took watch while I got some rest. About 5:00 a.m. the crew member on watch woke me up and said, 'Grant, you better come look at this.' I went to the pilothouse and immediately knew why he got me up. The seas were really building. During the course of the night we had drifted southeast off the Bank. I told the guys to secure the boat. Then we headed northwest and got back on the Bank not far from Lydonia Canyon to wait out the storm."

When the Mayday call came in around 3:00 p.m., Grant had trouble hearing it through all the static. But there was no mistaking Peter's voice. Grant had talked with Peter a couple of times that morning as well as with Billy Garnos on the *Fair Wind*, and he had a good idea of Peter's location. He stayed on the radio until he got the exact location of the *Sea Fever*, and then told Peter he was on his way.

"Thank God," says Grant, "that we were not to

Peter's south or east because we could not have made any headway at all going into those seas. It was scary as heck trying to get to him, and I knew I was putting my crew at risk, but Peter would have done the same for us. We were taking the seas on our port stern, and we were running as fast as we could. I had a couple guys just looking out at the incoming waves. They would holler if they saw a really big one, then I'd turn into it. After it went by, we'd get back on track. It was the worst weather any of us had ever seen. The *Broadbill* was making sounds we'd never even heard before. And the wind going through the rigging made a screaming noise that I'll never forget. Our pilot-house windows had a little visor over them, and as the waves came at us, we couldn't see their tops. They were absolute mountains."

Grant radioed the Coast Guard to make sure they had heard Peter's Mayday, which they had. But the nearest cutter was the *Active*, more than 150 miles away, and helicopters could not fly into the eighty-seven-knot winds tearing over the Bank.

The only boat that could help the *Sea Fever* was the *Broadbill*. Grant wondered if his vessel—just eighteen feet longer than the *Sea Fever*—could make it to Peter without becoming another casualty of the storm.

Grant Moore pushed the *Broadbill* as fast as he dared into the mountainous waves. He was well aware that in the span of a second he could switch from potential rescuer to victim. Should something go wrong—such as springing a hatch, catching a wave broadside, or being hit by a rogue wave—it would be disastrous. There were no other boats in the vicinity to come to his aid.

Although Grant was just fifteen miles from Peter and the *Sea Fever* when he first heard the Mayday, an hour had gone by, and he was still five miles away. Every ten to fifteen minutes he radioed Peter to hang on, that he and his crew were making progress but the seas made the going slow.

In the back of Grant's mind he struggled with two bleak questions: *What are we going to do when we get there, and what will we find?* He was amazed that the *Sea Fever*, with a third of its pilothouse blown away and in splinters, had not capsized. Even if the boat was afloat when he arrived, Grant already knew a vessel-to-vessel transfer of the crew was out of the question. To bring the vessels that close meant they might crash into each other or the survivors would fall between them during the exit.

———————✦———————

"When we got to where Peter was supposed to be," recalls Grant, "we couldn't see the *Sea Fever* anywhere. We kept shouting into the radio, 'Give us your position again!' We should have been right near them, and I'm thinking, *Where are they?* Then we were coming down off a wave and there they were, right below us!"

To this day Grant doesn't know how he managed to avoid slamming into the *Sea Fever*, but somehow the *Broadbill* cleared Peter's boat by a couple of feet.

Now Grant would have to make a dangerous turn. While he waited for just the right moment to make the maneuver, he once again asked himself how he was going to get the *Sea Fever* crew safely aboard his boat.

Chapter 11

TUMBLING IN THE VOID

THE MEN STILL ALIVE ON THE *SEA FEVER* HAD TWO things going for them that Ernie did not: they had one another and help was on the way. Ernie, on the other hand, floating in the raft, remained utterly alone, and no one even knew the *Fair Wind* had pitchpoled. Although the *Fair Wind* had been equipped with an emergency position-indicating rescue beacon, it apparently failed to send a signal.

The beacon may have needed to be manually activated, or if it did send a signal, the distress call was never heard. In 1980 the device was still in its infancy and often failed to activate during accidents. At that time the technology relied on aircraft to pick up the signal, rather than the satellites it uses today. The modern emergency beacon sends a signal that can be instantly identified through an encoded transmission program run by the National Oceanic and Atmospheric Administration. Vital information about the vessel and its location is passed to the Coast Guard. The modern beacon has a homing device so that rescue aircraft can pinpoint it, even on a drifting boat.

If Ernie's ordeal occurred today, he would likely be rescued within hours. That day, however, neither the Coast Guard nor the other boats on the Bank realized the *Fair Wind* had capsized. Of course, Ernie didn't know whether the beacon on the *Fair Wind* had sent a signal or not. Nor did he dwell on it because he was fighting for survival on a minute-by-minute basis, simply trying to make correct decisions as each new obstacle was thrown at him.

Now, at approximately 1:00 p.m., Ernie huddled inside the raft, still tethered to the *Fair Wind*. Chilled to the bone, he continued to endure the onslaught of breaking waves as the eighty-six-knot winds shrieked overhead and the wind-raked ocean thundered and roared. The sea was like an angry beast, enraged that one of the *Fair Wind*'s crew had escaped a watery grave. Now, it seemed, the ocean was intent on claiming Ernie one way or another.

As terrifying as the waves were, Ernie's bigger concern was that the *Fair Wind* would suddenly sink, dragging the raft to the bottom of the sea. The tether connecting the raft to the boat was designed to break free if the boat sank, but Ernie didn't know that, nor was there any guarantee that the line would perform as designed. He knew only that the line was very secure because it had not yet parted from the boat even with all the yanking by the wind and waves.

Around forty-five minutes after Ernie first climbed into the raft, he noticed that the *Fair Wind* had settled much lower in the water and only a small section of its hull was visible. Yet still he hesitated to release the raft. Even if his crewmates were dead—a reality that he was coming reluctantly to accept—he wondered if unfastening the raft was the right thing to do. To set himself loose from the boat was a huge decision. He knew all too well that once the raft became free, it would immediately be carried away from the boat, taking him into the void of endless gray ocean.

The raft was equipped with a small paddle, but

Ernie knew it would be useless as long as the storm raged. His mind raced, churning like the seas around him. The boat had taken on the same significance as the bucket he had clung to earlier—it represented a bit of security, something from his past, something before this misery—and he didn't want to let it go.

Maybe the boat will stay up a little longer, he thought. *I've always heard to stay with the boat as long as possible.* Once again he peered outside at the *Fair Wind*. Now the hull had nearly vanished. Ernie could not postpone the inevitable any longer, and he forced his fingers to untie the bowline knot.

Released from the *Fair Wind*, Ernie was met with a terrifying new sensation. The high, jagged waves instantly snatched the raft, lifting it up and over the wave crests and spinning it from side to side. Sometimes the raft couldn't make it over the waves. Instead it went halfway up before the top of the wave caved in on itself, burying the raft under tons of water. The breaking seas smacked Ernie's head and back, sending him sprawling face down on the floor of the raft. Amazingly, despite the nonstop frenetic motion, he did not get seasick.

Ernie's immediate concern was how to brace

himself for the waves that continually struck the raft; he worried their force could break his back. He tried lying on the floor, spread-eagle, as well as sitting with his feet out in front of him and his arms held toward the sides of the canopy. He was still experimenting with different positions when disaster struck. A wave slammed the raft with such fury that it knocked the raft on its side.

Ernie felt himself thrown free from his lifesaving capsule. He was now underwater, totally disoriented, and desperate for air. Opening his eyes, he saw the surface above him, and he furiously kicked his way up. He emerged in the foam bare chested, the wave having ripped away his sweatshirt. Fortunately, the raft was just a few feet away, and Ernie swam with every ounce of strength to reach it before the next wave broke upon him. He clawed his way into the doorway and collapsed on the floor, shaking.

Hearing the roar of another wave bearing down on him, Ernie positioned himself as best he could, determined to stay in the raft. Two straps inside walls of the raft served as handholds, and with a viselike grip he vowed not to let go. He even considered trying to somehow lash himself to the tiny vessel but quickly dismissed the idea, worried that if the raft tipped over completely he would drown inside. Ernie didn't know how much more he could take, but he was not going to let it end without fighting back. *I may die*, he thought, *but I'm not going to help it. As long as this raft floats, I'm staying with it.*

Losing his sweatshirt was yet another blow. Although it was soaking wet, it had provided an extra layer between Ernie's body and the seas, helping to trap a small amount of body heat, which would now dissipate immediately. A foot of water was sloshing inside the raft, and Ernie sat with his back against the canopy wall, facing the doorway, with his legs spread in front of him.

Ernie couldn't help but wonder how long the raft would hold up against the onslaught. How long would it be before one of the air chambers ripped and sprang a leak? As soon as that thought entered his consciousness, he forced himself to forget it, to just be ready for whatever happened next. He had to focus on what he could control, and that was himself. He could not dwell on the countless ways he might meet his end, but instead he told himself, *Fight. Hang in there. Just a few more hours and this storm will have moved on. Then the* Sea Fever *or the* Broadbill *will find me. And if not them, then the Coast Guard will have planes looking for me.* It was probably fortunate that Ernie didn't know about the *Sea Fever*'s own desperate situation.

Two hours had passed since the accident. Ernie had been in the storm so long that he barely noticed the shriek of the wind or the roar of the waves—but he felt their every move, and he tried leaning one way, then another, to keep the raft as stable as possible. He was learning to react to the waves, to anticipate their impact and brace himself as much as possible. Holding on to the straps proved exhausting. He noticed that his fingers had gone numb and cramped. Those hands, so strong from hauling gear all year, felt like rigid claws from his nonstop stranglehold on the straps.

Just a few minutes after Ernie reentered the raft, terror struck again. As he rose to the top of a huge charging wave, the wind caught the raft at just the right angle and sent it tumbling like a paper bag blown over an empty parking lot. The raft careened down the wave and came to rest upside down with Ernie still inside.

The small space that had saved Ernie's life now

entombed him, just as the *Fair Wind* had when it pitchpoled. Once again he found himself in darkness, underwater, with barely any air in his lungs. And, as before, his brain was screaming, *Get out, get out!*

He immediately groped around the sides of the canopy until he found the opening and swam out. Surfacing next to the overturned raft, coughing and spitting up seawater into his dripping black beard, he grabbed at the raft's bottom and hung on to the ballast bag as the seas crashed down on him.

Now that the raft was upside down, its living space was filled with water and acted as a ballast of its own, keeping the raft in that inverted position. Ernie had a sickening feeling that the raft would never right itself. He knew he no longer had the strength to turn it on his own. Such an effort might cause him to lose his grip. Without the little lifesaving capsule, the waves and frigid water would make short work of Ernie, dragging him down into the abyss of an uncaring sea.

As the waves tore at the overturned raft, Ernie mustered a bit of strength and crawled onto the bottom. Although his body was now mostly out of the water, his flesh, raw and red, was exposed to the hurricane-force winds and spray. His hands were almost completely numb and what was left of their gripping power weakened with each passing minute.

Ernie longed to put his hands under his armpits to warm them a bit, but he dared not let go of the raft. Eyeing the collapsed ballast bag next to him, the battered and bruised survivor snaked his way inside and squirmed into the fetal position. The bag was partially filled with water, but it shielded him from the wind and provided a relatively secure place to stay with the raft for whatever the seas had in store for him next.

A tear in the raft's ballast bag likely caused the raft to overturn. Ernie's concern for his friends inside the flipped *Fair Wind* and his earlier reluctance to set the raft adrift meant that the raft had remained tethered to the boat for almost an hour. The constant yanking on the tether may have ripped the ballast bag, or perhaps the sheer size of the seas had damaged the raft. Whatever the cause, the ballast bag, designed to keep the raft in an upright position, was slightly torn. When the storm knocked the raft on its side, water escaped from the bag through this tear.

Still, the Givens raft was arguably the best life

raft on the market at that time. Upon inflation, other life rafts, without the unique ballast bag, would have become airborne like a kite on a string until the wind ripped them to shreds. The raft that had so far saved Ernie from the seas was the invention of Jim Givens of Tiverton, Rhode Island. Givens came up with the idea for the unique ballast bag while serving in Korea as a paratrooper. "I met several fighter pilots whose buddies had died after ditching in the sea because their raft kept turning over. On my next jump, I looked up at my parachute and thought, I don't know why there couldn't be one of these at the bottom of a life raft." After his hitch in the service was up, Givens bounced around from job to job and even prospected for gold in California, but he couldn't escape the idea of a raft with an inverted parachute at the bottom. His goal to create an "unflippable" raft became an obsession. For years Givens sketched various designs of the raft's mechanical components, making dozens of revisions.

It wasn't until 1974 that Givens finally produced and sold his first raft, and orders for more quickly followed. "I didn't go to Harvard," said Givens, "and I'm not polished, but what I'm doing is right."

Givens's determination to make and market the

safest life raft possible was one reason Ernie was still alive. But the writhing sea and its hammering waves seemed intent on breaching the raft's thin fabric walls.

Despite everything Ernie had gone through, he responded to each new horror with controlled action rather than panic. He focused on the reality of his situation—not what might or might not happen—and reacted to each new peril as intelligently as he could. In a curious way, his boyhood made him better able to cope with the situation. He had not been coddled as a child, and that spurred his independence, just as his toughness likely grew from a childhood without many material possessions. Living in the back of a gas station for a few months as a teenager had given him a lesson in autonomy and street smarts far beyond his years. His stint in the army added to his self-confidence, as did his solo bike ride down the length of the West Coast. Despite the fact that he never went to college, he was a problem-solver with a curious mind.

Now, as before, he took advantage of what the situation offered—in this case the shelter of the torn ballast bag.

Chapter 12

INSIDE A PUNCHING BAG

In mile after endless mile of storm-tossed ocean, Ernie's orange life raft was the only speck of color. It was as if he had been kidnapped, put inside a capsule, and shot into space. No one even knew the *Fair Wind* had run into trouble because Billy had not been allowed any time to send a Mayday. No one knew Ernie had fought to survive yet was now in desperate need of help.

The *Fair Wind* was not scheduled to return to port for another four or five days, and perhaps nobody would become alarmed until it was overdue. By then it would be too late. If Ernie was never found, his friends and family would think it had ended quickly for him, never knowing about his courageous struggle.

For Ernie, the previous two hours had seemed almost as long as his entire life. The raft was upside down with Ernie curled up in the ballast bag, and both he and the raft were taking a tremendous pounding. It was almost as if Ernie was inside a punching bag being slugged by a giant, unseen fist. Ernie couldn't throw a punch back, so he had taken the only strategy available: outlast his opponent.

He was shivering uncontrollably, and he involuntarily tightened his arms around his knees each time a new wave was about to strike. The wait between each wave was about twenty seconds. Most of the waves were uniform in power and height, but every now and then a much stronger one came barreling toward Ernie. It was just such a wave that lifted the raft up toward its crest and then collapsed on it. The raft rolled yet again.

Now Ernie was trapped beneath the raft inside the fully submerged ballast bag. He had only seconds to escape before the next wave buried him deeper. He fought his way free, kicked to the surface, and crawled inside the raft's protective shell.

Gasping for air, eyes stinging, and freezing to the point of numbness, Ernie did not curse, but instead considered himself fortunate that the raft had righted itself without throwing him aside. He willed his body to get back into a sitting position with his legs spread toward the doorway.

He was on a roller coaster that could not be turned off. The seas carried him sixty feet up, then he slid sixty feet down, mountains and valleys, mountains and valleys. As the raft rode up and over each wave, Ernie experimented leaning one way and then the other, slowly getting the hang of actually controlling the raft so that the doorway faced away from the onrushing seas. Continually drenched, he found this little bit of steering helped to keep new water from coming inside.

Between waves Ernie bailed with his hands or with the raft's small paddle, as much to keep his circulation moving as to rid the raft of some of the water. Shivering, he thought about the sweatshirt he had lost and the jacket he had discarded in his effort to keep his head above the foam and waves when the *Fair Wind* first pitchpoled.

The winds were still screaming out of the north-west at velocities just better than eighty-six knots. Ernie knew he was being pushed southeastward toward the edge of Georges Bank, but he had no way of knowing what his drift rate was. He hoped it was slower than it felt. He knew that the farther he drifted from the *Fair Wind*'s last position, the harder it would be for rescuers to find him. He still held out hope that the emergency beacon had gone off and that Peter on the *Sea Fever* would come searching.

Although Ernie did his best to keep the raft's doorway from facing the oncoming waves, water continued to pour into the tiny craft. He considered tying the door flap shut. *But if I do that*, he thought, *I might not be able to get out if it flips upside down again*. He weighed the pros and cons of this action, just as he had when he considered lashing himself to the inside of the raft. He came to the conclusion that he needed the option of swimming free should the raft capsize again. It was ironic that the very raft designed to save him could also drown him. He could even die in the raft while it was right side up—a single wave, if it crashed directly on his head, could knock him unconscious. He'd likely drown in the foot of water at the bottom of the raft.

Just as Ernie thought he was doing a better job of controlling the raft and keeping its door away from the onslaught, an enormous wave lifted the vessel. Then the wall of water crashed down on it, smothering the raft. Ernie, spread-eagle inside, felt himself being pushed upside down, and was suspended that way for a long second. But the raft continued turning, completing a 360-degree roll. Ernie came up coughing and hacking, but he was still inside the tiny vessel.

Each wave was taking its toll as he braced himself for the next one, never knowing if it would be the one that would tear the raft apart. His body had been producing adrenaline almost nonstop since the *Fair Wind* pitchpoled, and it was a wonder he hadn't given up from pure exhaustion.

Ernie was no more than a tiny cork in the ocean, but a single-minded cork whose primary thought was just to survive the next wave. Every now and then, in the troughs of a wave, he risked shifting position so that he could quickly peek out the doorway. He hoped to spot one of the other fishing boats. But he saw only a mountain of water so tall it blocked the horizon and muffled the sound of the wind that raged above. Yellow-gray spume flew through the air. He was totally alone.

Chapter 13

TRAPPED

BRAD, SARGE, AND PETER, STILL ABOARD THE *SEA Fever*, had adopted a mindset much like Ernie's: survive the next wave. After losing Gary and issuing the Mayday, the three men donned survival suits. They prayed that Grant Moore aboard the *Broadbill* would arrive before the *Sea Fever* went down.

"We were in a real bind," recalls Peter, "because if we tried to go into the seas, the waves would have continued to come through the broken windshield. On the other hand, if we went with the seas, the same surfing and then broaching would happen like when we lost Gary. We knew either one of those positions would get us killed. So we laid to (let the boat drift) with the engine in neutral because there simply weren't any other options, and we were still afloat. The waves were hitting our port side, which was how we wanted to take them since the starboard side of our pilothouse was in pieces." And so Peter no longer steered the boat, but let the *Sea Fever* be carried sideways by the waves.

Peter didn't know it, but the wooden ribs in the boat's hull were beginning to crack, adding more water to what had already come in through the blown windows and the shattered side of the pilothouse. The pilothouse contained a hand pump, a device that looked somewhat like the kind seen on an old well. The men took turns working the pump between waves, keeping up with the water collecting in the bilge but never seeming to get ahead of it.

A more serious concern than the incoming water, however, was the size of the waves now slamming into and nearly engulfing the boat. Some were so large that the men feared being flushed out of the boat through the same shattered opening Gary had crashed through, and they soon abandoned pumping to get into safer positions.

They found that the most secure location was the floor of the pilothouse. They sat with their backs against the port wall and their feet braced against the engine room box, which rose up two feet near the center of the pilothouse.

"We would hear each wave coming at us," says Brad, "and the roaring got louder each second. When the wave hit the port side, it would tip the boat to an almost ninety-degree angle, and we'd be looking straight down at the smashed opening on the starboard side and see a mass of churning water. If our feet lost their grip on the engine room box, we would have been hurled down into that opening, and that would be the end. The boat would surf down the breaking wave, and it was just a thunderous, crashing noise, and we would be surrounded by white water. The energy was so strong, I really thought the waves would crack the boat like an egg. Then, when the wave passed beneath us, I'd let my breath out, and we would rock back into the trough. The boat would stabilize a bit, and we'd await the next wave. By raising our heads we could see the oncoming wave approach through the port window, and they were as tall as trees. I just had this awful, sinking pit in my stomach watching or hearing the wave approach. And it was physically exhausting trying to keep in the same position. The only thing that kept me going was pure adrenaline coursing through me."

Sarge recalls the harrowing experience with equal clarity. "I really thought that the next big wave was going to knock us so far on our side that we wouldn't come up. And I was worried the radio would die with all the water coming into the boat. Even though Peter got the Mayday off, I wasn't sure Grant would be able to find us. I wanted to get off that boat as quickly as possible, and we talked about what we would do if and when Grant came. We discussed using a rope to tie the three of us in a line so no one would get separated when we went in the water. I was thinking Grant could shoot a line over and haul us through the water with their lobster winch. We all agreed we were going to get off the boat the second Grant arrived."

During that agonizing wait for help, Sarge also made a vow that if he lived, the very first thing he would do was go to church. He hadn't been in years, but he thought that should he survive, it would be nothing less than a miracle. Peter feared they were only minutes from death.

"The waves put us down to rail level," recalls Peter, "then just scooted us along at incredible speeds, just like we were going over a waterfall. I remember how we shouted to each other about how we'd tie ourselves together with plenty of line in between us, and then Grant could haul us in. The main thing was that after what had just happened with Gary, we were going to do this together—either we'd all make it or we'd all die. Because we had our survival suits on we even considered not waiting for Grant, and instead jumping over together immediately. That's how certain we were that the boat was going to roll completely over on the next big wave and we'd be trapped inside. But then I remembered my father shouting, 'Stay with the boat no matter what,' so we decided to follow his advice."

Peter couldn't help thinking back to the start of the trip. Unlike the crew of the *Fair Wind*, Peter had been reluctant to violate the old fisherman's superstition that warned about setting out on a Friday. But he knew his father would never allow a superstition to get in the way of fishing, and so Peter never even mentioned it. Now Gary was gone, and Peter and the rest of his crew seemed likely to suffer the same bleak fate at any minute.

About three hours after the *Sea Fever*'s terrifying ordeal began, Grant's *Broadbill* finally arrived. The crew of the *Sea Fever* first spotted the *Broadbill* on the crest of a wave high above them. Suddenly it careened down the face of the wave, nearly plowing into the *Sea Fever*.

On the one hand, the survivors were relieved that Grant had found them, but the sight of Grant's boat made them realize the waves were even taller and more violent than they'd thought. This plunged them into a deeper despair. The ocean tossed the sixty-five-foot *Broadbill* as easily as a toy. One second the *Broadbill* would soar high above the *Sea Fever*'s crew, its propellers briefly visible in the foam, and the next minute they'd be looking down on the *Broadbill*, spray and rain sweeping over its deck. Still, so desperate were the men on the *Sea Fever* that they considered following through with their plan to jump into the sea.

Peter radioed Grant and shouted that the *Sea Fever* seemed about to go down and that they were preparing to jump off. Grant yelled back not to make a move, that he'd swing around and try to get closer, and then they'd figure out what to do.

Grant turned the *Broadbill*, but the action proved so violent he radioed Peter again almost immediately, "If you're really going to jump, I'll try and get you, but I'm telling you I don't think you're going to make it. We will end up killing you guys. You'll get crushed. Just look at the action of my stern."

Peter knew Grant was right, and so did Sarge and Brad. "I couldn't wait to get off," says Sarge, "but I could see the way the waves were crashing against the hull of the *Broadbill*, and it didn't look good. I thought we might not survive being pulled alongside and instead be killed by slamming into his steel hull. It seemed cruel to have help so close but still be trapped on the boat."

The tension, Brad recalls, was unbearable. "I had put all my hopes into Grant getting us off the boat, and now I could see that might not work. At nineteen years old I was terrified, and I just tried to keep my emotions in check and let Peter and Grant make the right decision. With each wave I'm thinking there's a large chance I'm going to die. That feeling, over and over, is just awful. And here was another boat just sixty feet away, and yet we couldn't get off. If the *Sea Fever* went all the way over—and it sure felt like it would—there wasn't a thing Grant and his crew could do. We'd die right in front of him, trapped in the pilothouse, where we would be drowned."

Chapter 14

THE COAST GUARD

About the only people in New England who knew that a storm of titanic proportions was raging at Georges Bank were those working at the US Coast Guard's regional headquarters in Boston. Throughout the morning Lieutenant Robert Eccles had juggled no fewer than eight search and rescue operations, including four "sinkers." From the operations center, he and his fellow Coasties, as they often call themselves, had directed a number of successful rescues without any loss of life. Then they received the Mayday from the *Sea Fever*.

Eccles knew that a crew member had been swept off the boat and now worried that the remaining crew members would not survive long enough for the *Broadbill* or the cutter *Active* to reach them. He alerted Air Station Cape Cod to attempt to send a helicopter to the scene, though he knew the high winds might make it impossible to send one any time soon.

Safe in the confines of his office, Eccles felt a sense of helplessness hearing the details of the emergency without being able to do anything physically to help. During his tenure in the Coast Guard, Eccles had come to the conclusion that talking to people in Mayday situations was often much more draining than being involved in the actual on-scene search and rescue. "There have been times," recalls Eccles, "when I'd be talking to fishermen on the radio, and I knew they were going to die within minutes. One of the worst times was talking to two men aboard a fishing vessel sinking off Gloucester in the winter. They radioed in their Mayday, and I dispatched patrol boats to assist them, but it would take a while for them to reach the fishing boat. The two men said the boat was sinking lower by the second. I asked if they had their life jackets on, and they responded that they did. Then I asked if they had their survival suits on and they said, 'No, they're down below.' That's when

I knew I was talking to dead men. It was going to take them a good five minutes or more to get those suits and get them on, and by that time the boat would be submerged. They had to abandon ship immediately, and I knew they wouldn't last in the water more than a few minutes, not nearly long enough for our boats to get there. When our vessels got on site, the fishing boat was gone and so were the men."

Eccles had several years of experience coordinating difficult rescues, but nothing had prepared him for what was happening at Georges Bank.

While Ernie and the men aboard the *Sea Fever* struggled to stay alive, their families and loved ones had no idea of their plight. In a sad twist of fate, Maria Pavlis, fiancée of *Fair Wind* captain Billy Garnos, was shopping for her wedding dress in Boston at approximately the same time the *Fair Wind* pitchpoled and Billy drowned.

Maria had met Billy through his sister in the early 1970s, when Maria was a teacher and Billy had just been drafted into the army and was soon to be sent to Vietnam. Maria had her second-grade students write to Billy, hoping that the letters would make him laugh and give him some comfort so far away from home. When Billy returned from Vietnam, he continued to be the bighearted, fun-loving guy he was before he left. He rarely mentioned Vietnam and didn't volunteer any information about the combat he saw. But some friends knew he'd seen plenty. In fact, one friend, fishing boat captain Hugh Bishop, found out the hard way. Hugh had hired Billy as a deckhand on his fifty-foot fishing vessel, the *Mistress*, and they made two-day trips out of Marblehead, line-trawling for groundfish. On one of the overnight trips Hugh went down to wake Billy up for his turn on watch and got quite a surprise. "No sooner did I put my hand on his shoulder," says Hugh, "than Billy grabbed my throat in a viselike grip. He had come from a dead sleep to having a stranglehold on me in half a second. Billy later explained it was because of what he'd been through in Vietnam. I made sure in the future that when I woke him, I hopped out of reach immediately."

Just before the Georges Bank accident, Billy and Maria had gotten engaged. Although they'd known each other for years, they did not connect romantically until the wedding of Billy's sister, Rose, who was a friend of Maria's, on September 6, 1980. "Something magical happened that day. It was as if we had always been together," says Maria. "We were engaged on November 11, 1980, and planned to be married on February 14, 1981. It was such a short time, but I had never been happier, and in my heart I know that Billy was just as happy."

Chapter 15

A SILENT KILLER

ERNIE'S SITUATION HAD CHANGED LITTLE AS THE afternoon progressed and the storm maintained its intensity. Over the course of the day he had swallowed a fair amount of seawater, which only increased his mounting thirst from the exertion required to stay inside the raft. He could see a survival bag tied to the inside walls of the raft, and between waves he glanced inside the bag, noting it contained flares, a pump, and cookies. Most important, he saw six cans of water. He dared not remove a can of water from the bag for fear the seas would sweep it out the door. He could go awhile longer without the precious liquid.

Ernie had now been subjected to more than three hours of torture, and the mental strain was unimaginable. In the blink of an eye his world had collapsed. He had lost his friends, his boat, and nearly his life. In an uncaring sea, he was a mere speck in mile after mile of raging white water.

Most people would have cracked under such pressure, but Ernie still focused on each problem as it arose. And there was absolutely no room for error. At each moment when action was called for, he had to get every decision right without discussing his reasoning with anyone else. He was being put through a mental and physical test, where he couldn't score a 98 or 99 percent. To live, he had to score 100 percent.

Ernie's teeth were chattering, his lips blue, his flesh waterlogged, and his stamina flagging. The waves assaulting his raft had managed to swallow the fifty-foot steel-hulled *Fair Wind*. What chance did he have with only one-eighth of an inch of rubberized fabric separating him from the roaring sea? The waves were unrelenting; it would have been so easy to give up and just slip away, ending the nightmare quickly. But Ernie refused.

About an hour before sunset an especially strong wave ambushed Ernie yet again. Thousands of pounds of surging seawater slammed into his head and back. The raft tipped on end so that the doorway faced directly downward. With diminished strength, Ernie clutched the canopy straps, holding his breath. He tried to use his legs to keep from falling through the doorway.

Fortunately, the raft continued rolling, completing a 360-degree turn as the rest of the frothing wave slid beneath Ernie. Remarkably, when the raft returned to its upright position, enough water flooded back into the ballast bag to keep the raft from getting rolled by the next chaotic wave. Water cascaded out of the raft, leaving only a foot or two sloshing at the bottom. Ernie steeled himself for the next wave and pushed the canopy back into place.

In addition to the waves, another enemy was working against Ernie: hypothermia. This silent killer was making inroads against Ernie's body, as he was losing more heat than he could generate. If his body's core temperature dropped to 87 degrees, he would lose consciousness and die.

Ernie was now well into the initial stages of hypothermia. His body had begun to shiver violently in an effort to increase body heat. The shivering, however, was having little effect because half of his body was submerged in the 55-degree water sloshing around inside the raft. During the brief lulls between waves he often tried to bail out some of the water using his small paddle. But Ernie could never remove the bottom six or seven inches covering the floor of the raft.

The air temperature at Georges Bank was about the same as the ocean's, but it was the water doing the damage, sucking away Ernie's body heat twenty-five times faster than the air. His extremities suffered most. The blood vessels in his hands and feet were beginning to contract, allowing less blood to flow through them. This reduced the amount of cold blood returning to his vital organs. The body's defense in these conditions is to relinquish the hands and feet to the cold in an effort to concentrate the diminishing warmth in the inner core and the vital organs.

If the hypothermia advanced, blood flow to Ernie's arms and legs would also decrease. The rate of heat loss varies slightly among individuals, primarily due to body fat. Ernie was six feet tall, 195 pounds, and most of that was muscle rather than fat, thanks to his grueling work as a fisherman.

The raft's canopy was probably Ernie's best protection against hypothermia. The canopy's thin fabric helped to shield Ernie from the windchill, which speeds heat loss from the body. Unfortunately, the canopy was about all Ernie had to aid in his struggle against the cold. Heat loss also occurs through a person's head, and Ernie had no hat. His sweatshirt had been stripped away by the waves. All he had on was a pair of jeans and socks, but because they were both wet, they retained only a fraction of their insulating value.

Conserving energy is another way to slow the process of heat loss. Ernie, however, didn't have that luxury. His immediate concern was to keep himself in the raft and keep it upright, which required shifting and balancing. Despite all these problems, his situation was brighter than before he entered the raft.

———◆———

Peter, Sarge, and Brad—still trapped on the *Sea Fever*—had the benefit of survival suits, unlike Ernie.

Thanks to these specially designed suits, hypothermia was not an issue for the *Sea Fever* crew, but drowning remained a very real threat. If a wave caught the vessel just right, the port side, which was lifted to an almost ninety-degree angle on every wave, would continue all the way over, trapping the men inside. Their predicament would be much like the one faced by the crew of the *Fair Wind* when it pitchpoled.

Perhaps the broken windows and shattered starboard pilothouse wall of the *Sea Fever* would offer escape routes, but the survival suits might hinder the crew's movement. And if the *Sea Fever* capsized, the buoyancy of the survival suits would push the men up against the deck and into a temporary air pocket. If that happened, the survivors would be hard-pressed to descend and grope for an opening from the boat.

So far, however, the decision to let the boat lay to without power or steering and just surf sideways down the waves was working, if just by a matter of inches. Peter could not turn the boat into the seas because the windshields were gone, and he had already tried running in the same direction as the waves, with disastrous consequences. All three men agreed the best course of action was to continue to let the boat ride the liquid mountains on its own. They had to stay in their cramped sitting position with their feet braced against the engine block, or they'd slide into the abyss on the starboard side. In the survival suits, with the mitten hands, it would be impossible to grab anything to stop the slide.

Grant Moore, on the *Broadbill*, watched the *Sea Fever* with amazement. The wounded vessel surfed down the face of each towering wave, propelled by a boiling fury of foam and seawater. "I could see how low the *Sea Fever* was riding in the water," says Grant, "but there was nothing we could do except stand off as close as we could. So I put my stern off his bow and just clutched in and out of gear trying to stay as close as possible."

Grant's situation was akin to that of an airport traffic controller who is helpless to free passengers from an incoming plane with mechanical trouble. The controller might have a visual on the plane and give advice over the radio, but all he or she can really do to help is order emergency teams and equipment to stand by. In Grant's situation, he had both a visual on the *Sea Fever* and radio communication, and now he stood by, ready to respond if the worst happened.

On the *Sea Fever* the roar of the waves muffled most other sounds, but Peter still heard the boat make some noises he'd never heard before. Occasionally the boat would groan as if it were alive and in its final throes of agony. Other times he thought he heard sharp cracks coming from below. Peter strained to listen, wondering if the wooden spine and ribs of the vessel were coming apart faster than he suspected. There was so much gear crashing around below in the galley and bunkroom it was impossible for him to know.

To go below would be suicide—a death trap because if the boat did capsize, he'd never escape. "There was nothing we could do now except wait it out," recounts Peter. "And I don't think Sarge, Brad, and I said more than a few words to each other."

The crew grieved over the loss of Gary and tried to hold back their fear they would not survive the afternoon. "The waiting was unbearable," Brad recalls. "It was just agony, never knowing if the next wave was going to finish us off. I'd put all my hopes into the *Broadbill* saving us and now we had to hang on indefinitely."

Chapter 16

A PILOT'S NIGHTMARE

HELICOPTER PILOTS BUCK BALEY AND JOE TOUZIN were exhausted. Throughout the day on Saturday, November 22, 1980, they had flown mission after mission from Air Station Cape Cod to vessels in distress up and down the New England coast. Now, at approximately 4:30 p.m., with the sun already set, rescue coordinators determined that the winds over Georges Bank had abated slightly. They decided to attempt a helicopter rescue of the men aboard the crippled *Sea Fever.*

"We had a crew of four," says Baley, "and all of us were just beat. We had logged a lot of air time, flying to one case after another near Cape Cod. The trip to Georges Bank had us concerned."

Touzin concurs, adding, "A round trip to Georges Bank was approximately 325 miles with a half hour allowed for our on-scene work. We knew we would be at the max of the chopper's fuel limit, so after we launched about 4:30 p.m., we made a brief stop at Nantucket to top off our tanks. After that, as we headed for Georges Bank, I couldn't help but think about a helo crash with fatalities a year earlier."

Touzin and Baley had good reason to be concerned. The helicopter accident that lingered in the backs of their minds occurred under conditions eerily similar to the ones the two pilots now faced. In that accident four of the five crew members perished during a winter night rescue on Georges Bank. No one will ever know for sure what caused the calamity, but investigators theorized that either the engines ingested salt water, causing them to fail, or ice formed on the chopper's shell, destabilizing it.

Pilots Baley and Touzin tried not to think about their friends who died in that accident, but found it impossible. Adding to their concern was a deep weariness from the already hectic day and an uncertainty about what kind of conditions they'd find out at Georges Bank. Although the winds had eased from hurricane force, they'd heard frightening reports about incredible wave heights of seventy feet. All they knew was that the *Sea Fever* had lost a man overboard and the vessel was foundering after having its windows blown out.

"Flying out," says Baley, "we were really watching our fuel gauges, thinking about the return trip. Winds were coming out of the northwest, assisting us on the trip to the emergency, but we'd be flying into them on the flight home. We were streaking right along, anxious to make radio contact with the crippled vessel or one of the other fishing vessels that was standing by."

Baley was the aircraft commander for the flight and sat in the pilot's seat on the right side of the HH-3F helicopter, while Touzin was in the copilot seat. The two men, however, took turns actually piloting the helicopter, a standard practice. Because it was late November, both men worried about icing—the disastrous effects of ice buildup on the rotors. Consequently, they flew the chopper lower than an airplane would have gone, hoping to avoid the ice by staying in the relatively warmer temperatures near the ocean's surface.

Also on board was navigator Tony Davern, who sat in the back of the chopper and operated the electronic navigation system, making sure they stayed on course while at the same time staying in contact with the Coast Guard operations center in Boston. Tony describes the mission as "task saturated" because the weather was so bad that it kept the crew extremely busy. He made sure he monitored their distance from Nantucket and Long Island as they proceeded. He wanted to know exactly where the nearest point of land was in case of an emergency. A fourth crew member, whose name could not be recalled, would operate the rescue hoist to lift up the fishermen once the helicopter reached the *Sea Fever*. (There was no rescue swimmer on board because in 1980 that position had not yet been established.)

The closer the helicopter got to the *Sea Fever*, the worse the conditions became, and the wind buffeted the HH-3F. Neither Baley nor Touzin felt comfortable with the mission. They had been flying all day, and they worried that their reflexes were not as sharp as they should have been. The pilots needed to stretch and to rest. In the cramped cockpit, however, surrounded by instrument panels and equipment, they could do neither.

Wind gusts frequently pushed the helicopter off course. Both pilots worried about their ability to safely rescue men from a sinking boat in such terrific wind. How would they be able to hold a hovering position if they could barely stay in a straight line under full forward power? In the dark, trying to maintain a constant altitude just above the boat, there would be little to no visual reference points for the pilots. They would have to rely heavily on the hoist operator's instructions coming through their headsets. They would also need to be low enough for the basket to reach the pitching boat but not so low that the spray from the wave tops could reach their engine.

The hoist operator would have his own problems trying to control a wildly swinging rescue basket at the end of a wire cable. Waves would lift the boat close to the chopper as they crested, but then drop it low in the troughs. All the while, the chopper would be lurching from turbulence. The radio operator would be in the doorway as well, helping the hoist operator and offering another set of eyes alert to danger.

Every person on that helicopter would need to operate in a delicate, balanced, and coordinated way to be precise enough to pull off this rescue. And the crew of the *Sea Fever* would need to be as steady and decisive as possible to avoid disaster. If the survivors grabbed for the rescue basket too soon, they might miss and tumble off the boat. And if they failed to get hold of the basket at the right moment, the basket itself might slam into them and knock them overboard. Fishing them out of the water would be next to impossible. The chopper crew would have to lower the basket beneath the water's surface so the victim in the cumbersome survival suit could claw his way into it. At night this was a worst-case scenario. There was a real possibility that the pilots and hoist operator would be unable to locate the men in the midst of so much streaking foam and churning seas.

These thoughts raced through the minds of Baley and Touzin. Being cautious is part of what makes a good pilot, just as nervous tension keeps a person focused and alert. Of course, a pilot cannot let this apprehension turn into debilitating fear, which would in turn affect performance. Hours of training and years of actual experience help prevent this outcome.

Baley had logged close to two thousand hours of flight time in the Coast Guard, including a two-year tour in Kodiak, Alaska. The rugged, high terrain of the coastline provided additional challenges to night flying. Joe Touzin had Coast Guard flying experience as well as combat seasoning. He had been a captain in the marines, stationed on an aircraft carrier off the coast of Vietnam. In the closing days of that war, Joe flew chopper missions into Saigon to rescue people as the Vietcong and North Vietnamese entered the outskirts of the city. He understood pressure, and that understanding was going to help him in this rescue.

On board the *Sea Fever*, Sarge felt a glimmer of hope that he, Peter, and Brad were going to make it without ending up in the water. Sometime between 4:00 and 5:00 p.m. he noticed that the wind outside the pilothouse had decreased somewhat in intensity. The waves were every bit as ferocious as before. But for the first time since 5:00 that morning, Sarge felt convinced that the seas would not grow any larger. As night fell around the crippled boat, Sarge kept these thoughts to himself. He didn't want to speak too soon.

By 6:00 p.m. Sarge felt confident enough that he shouted to Brad and Peter, asking if they felt the wind had eased a little. They had been thinking the same thing but, like Sarge, were almost afraid that if they said anything too soon, they'd invite more fury from the storm.

Indeed the wind had slackened, but the men were only slightly relieved. Their muscles still tensed each time a new wave slammed the boat, and they wondered if the wooden vessel could continue to hold its own against the seas. So far, however, the boat had saved them from what looked like certain death just three hours earlier. They now realized that the decision to stay inside the *Sea Fever* instead of leaping into the water when the *Broadbill* arrived probably saved them from drowning or getting crushed by the *Broadbill*. And now they were thinking ahead to their next decision—what to do if and when a helicopter arrived.

Peter decided to raise his father on the radio again. He explained their predicament, and again Bob Brown's instructions were the same: to remain on the boat even if a helicopter arrived. He pointed out that the boat had already survived the worst of the storm, and if the *Sea Fever* had lasted this long, it would certainly carry them through the night. Bob had decades of experience on the sea, and he thought this course of action would be the safest. Of course, he also had the *Sea Fever* itself in mind—why abandon a vessel, equipment, and gear worth more than a hundred thousand dollars if they could be saved?

Bob added that just as soon as the size of the waves decreased, he would start pounding his way toward the *Sea Fever*. He estimated he'd be able to arrive sometime after dawn. "Just have the helicopter drop you a pump," Bob shouted into the radio, "and everything is going to be all right."

Peter agreed. They had resumed keeping up with the incoming water, and with a backup gasoline-powered pump from the Coast Guard he'd have another line of defense. He talked it over with Brad and Sarge, who also thought staying with the boat was better than trying to grab hold of a swinging rescue basket.

Peter raised Grant on the radio and told him of the decision to stay with the boat. Grant too agreed, saying he'd keep the *Broadbill* just off their bow through the night.

When Joe Touzin, Buck Baley, and Tony Davern were ten miles from the *Sea Fever*, they were able to raise

Peter on the radio and were relieved to learn that the crew had decided to stay with the boat. "We asked them if they wanted to get off," recalls Touzin, "but they elected to stay on board and asked us to lower a pump. That was probably the right decision because there's nothing easy about dropping and retrieving a rescue basket in high seas, strong winds, and at night. Any number of things can go wrong."

As the chopper sped toward the *Sea Fever*, the pilots began to explain to Peter how they would get the pump to the crew below. They could not simply lower the pump at the end of a line; that would swing like a wrecking ball. Instead the hoist operator would tie the pump to one end of a line, and the opposite end of the same line would be weighted. Then as the helo hovered as well as it could over the boat, the hoist operator would drop the weighted end of the line onto the boat, hoping it would land on the open deck behind the pilothouse. One of the crewmen would then have to go out on the deck and retrieve the line.

Next, the hoist operator would drop the pump, which was in a floating watertight canister, into the ocean. The men on the *Sea Fever* could haul the pump in. In theory, and in most situations, the plan was fairly easy to execute. At night, in sixty-foot seas with powerful wind gusts, it was anything but.

The chopper crew could now see the *Sea Fever* and the *Broadbill* on their radar whenever the boats came up out of the troughs. Arriving at the scene, the pilot flew strictly by instruments, and the copilot looked out the window until he saw the boat. Then they flicked on the helicopter's landing gear and searchlight. The pilots began coaxing the chopper into a lower position above the *Sea Fever*.

"The main thing going through my mind," says Baley, "was that we had to be low enough to be accurate dropping the line but high enough that we didn't get caught by a big sea—that would push the boat's rigging into the helo."

Everything was in constant motion—the boat, its rigging, the helicopter, and the seas. Tony Davern, the navigator, recalls that the boat was violently pitching and rolling. He worried about the men on board and their decision to stay, but he said to himself, *It's their boat and it's their lives.*

The whirling of the helicopter's main rotor blade was kicking foam into the air, and the pilots worried that the salt spray was entering the engines. The chopper's low hover position combined with the high wind meant that the engines were ingesting a small amount of salt water. Over time, salt deposits build up on the turbine blades on the intake side of the engine. This disrupts the airflow across those blades, and the engines begin to run hotter. "If the buildup of salt deposits continues," explains Baley, "the airflow is disrupted to the point that the engine could lose much of its power or even stall." It was therefore imperative that Baley's helicopter hover only briefly, which meant dropping the pump line accurately on the first try.

The hoist operator was responsible for directing the pilots into the perfect position so that he could make the drop. Speaking into the radio transmitter attached to his helmet, the hoist operator said, "Easy left," then "Forward, ten feet." He looked down and could see the stern of the *Sea Fever* directly below. The chopper was pointed into the wind, and he knew the line would be blown backward, so he again instructed the pilots to go forward another few feet. Then he dropped the line.

Sarge recalled how the lights from the helicopter illuminated the towering waves and whitecaps in an eerie glow. "Those Coast Guard guys were real pros," says Sarge. "On the first try they dropped that line right across the boat. I crawled out on the deck and grabbed it. Then they dropped the pump in the water right next to us and all we had to do was haul it in."

The pilots told the men below that they had just enough fuel to get back to Nantucket, but they'd make a quick search for Gary. They turned on their multimillion-candlepower light, the Night Sun, and started making wider and wider circles around the boat. Baley describes the search as follows: "It's as if you had to look for a silver dollar on a football field at night with a flashlight while riding a moped, and you only had a limited amount of time. I won't say it was impossible. We have found people at night with no reflective tape or strobe lights, but it sure was a long shot."

Down below, Peter, Brad, and Sarge knew that Gary was long since dead and that the pilots would never find him. As the roar of the helicopter's engine and the thumping of its rotors faded, the men on the *Sea Fever* wondered if they had made the right decision to stay with the boat through the night.

Part III

Chapter 17

ALONE IN THE NIGHT

ERNIE HAZARD NEVER NOTICED THAT THE WINDS had diminished slightly because the waves seemed just as enormous and their sound was still deafening. Most of the six-story waves continued to break on the raft's canopy, nearly crushing Ernie beneath their weight. Each time one struck, he had to quickly push the canopy back up to get the water off him.

Between waves Ernie's bearded chin often fell upon his breast in utter exhaustion, but rest was impossible. The robotic exertion it took to balance the tiny capsule went on and on.

But he still had his fight. At one point, out of pure frustration, he angrily screamed a challenge at the seas: "Is that the best you got?"

Nightfall was closing in on Ernie's violent and desolate world. He had been battling for survival within the raft for five straight hours, all the while hoping for the long shot that another fishing boat might spot him. He now understood that for another boat to have any chance at finding him, he would have to first hear or see the boat approaching and then fire off a flare. Rather than dwell on the fact that he could barely hear above the waves, he told himself that should he spot a boat, or even a plane, his flare might be seen.

Ernie could tell that the raft had lost some air, but the sea was too frenzied for him to pull the pump from the survival bag and use it. He refused to worry about the raft's structural integrity in the face of the onslaught because nothing could be done. He simply hoped the raft's designers had pictured sixty-foot waves when they chose the fabric and the sealant used to separate the air chambers. It was a good thing he didn't know that these same waves were cracking the oak ribs on the *Sea Fever* just a few miles away.

By 5:00 p.m. darkness had enveloped Ernie. The raft came equipped with a small red beacon on top of the canopy, but it had been ripped away in the first few minutes after the *Fair Wind* pitchpoled. It was as if he had lost his sense of sight. He forced himself to stay fully alert, for if the raft capsized now, he might not be able to maintain his grip on it. Should he become separated from the raft he would surely die. He refused to waver from the mindset he had adopted in the first hour of the ordeal—*I may die, but not without a fight.*

About an hour or two later Ernie's worst fear came true: a snarling wave flipped the raft completely upside down and the vessel did not continue its roll. For a split second Ernie's feet were pointed toward the surface and his head was underwater as the seas came flooding into the overturned raft, smothering him.

Ernie thrashed and kicked to find the opening. But in the darkness the task was tougher and more disorienting than it had been earlier. Precious seconds ticked by as he held his breath and swung his hands along the raft's wall to find the door. He could sense the water seething around him, holding the raft down the way a cat pounces on a mouse.

Suddenly Ernie was free from the raft. As he came up for air, the razor-sharp wind screamed around him, and immediately he felt its chilling bite. Groping and flailing wildly in the darkness, his hands at first felt nothing but foam and water. Finally, his fingers hit the raft and found the outside line that encircled it, which he clamped on to with a ferocious grip. He could not, would not, lose the raft.

Water cascaded from the ballast bag, which was now just above the ocean's surface. For a second Ernie thought about climbing atop the raft and trying to right it himself. But he quickly dismissed the idea and instead struggled to get inside the ballast bag and out of the wind. Now, on top of the upside-down raft and inside the ballast bag, he collapsed, panting and shaking from the effort and the cold.

Ernie kept his head at the opening of the ballast bag and gulped in big breaths of air and its precious oxygen. Then a terrifying thought sent an electric jolt through him: *Has the survival bag been washed out of the raft?* In it were the flares and the water he'd need to survive.

Rain pelted the ballast bag in violent torrents, and the waves battered Ernie with such ferocity that he was afraid they'd crack his back like a dried twig. Then he felt a wave slam the raft with such power that

LOCATION OF BOATS IN THE STORM

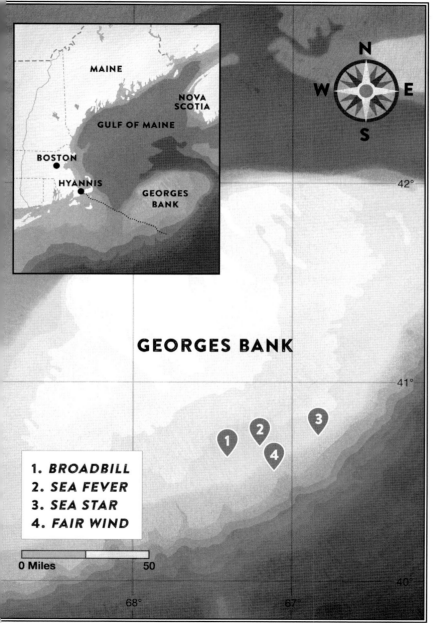

MAINE

NOVA SCOTIA

GULF OF MAINE

BOSTON

HYANNIS

GEORGES BANK

GEORGES BANK

42°

41°

1. *BROADBILL*
2. *SEA FEVER*
3. *SEA STAR*
4. *FAIR WIND*

0 Miles   50

40°

68°   67°

Art by Keith Robinson

On a calm, cold day in November 1980, the *Fair Wind*, a fifty-foot steel lobster boat, left Hyannis, Massachusetts, on what would be its final voyage.

Maria Pavlis/Billy Garnos

The *Sea Fever*, a forty-seven-foot wooden lobster boat battered and beaten by the ferocious storm, was owned by Bob Brown, who later bought the doomed *Andrea Gail*, made famous by Sebastian Junger's *The Perfect Storm*.

Peter M. Brown

(*Left*) Ernie Hazard, a tough three-year veteran of the *Fair Wind*'s crew, had never encountered waves as tall or as fierce as those he faced that day.

Maria Pavlis/Billy Garnos

(*Right*) Billy Garnos, the thirty-year-old captain of the *Fair Wind*, did not believe in taking unnecessary chances. Had he learned of the looming storm, he almost certainly would have delayed the trip.

Maria Pavlis/Billy Garnos

(*Left*) Twenty-two-year-old Rob Thayer of the *Fair Wind* was a rookie nearing the end of his first lobster-fishing season. As fate would have it, his first season would also be his last.

Maria Pavlis/Billy Garnos

(Right) At just twenty years old, Dave Berry was the youngest member of the *Fair Wind*'s ill-fated crew.

Nancy Antonich

(Left) Billy Garnos had recently gotten engaged. He was looking forward to becoming the captain of a bigger vessel than the *Fair Wind*.

Maria Pavlis/Billy Garnos

(Right) Peter Brown (left) and his father, Bob, were both swept up in the storm; twenty-three-year-old Peter captained the *Sea Fever*, and Bob, the *Sea Star*.

Peter M. Brown

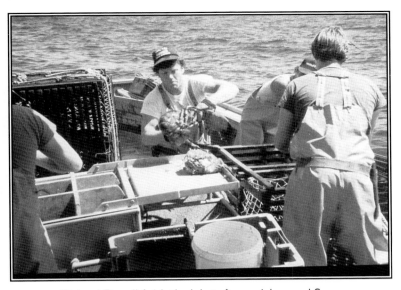

Richard Rowell (with the lobster) was nicknamed Sarge
because he was a twenty-three-year-old former marine.

Peter M. Brown

Sarge relished the demanding life of an offshore lobster
fisherman, which often called for twenty-hour days
spent heaving lobster traps on and off the deck.

Peter M. Brown

The raft and Ernie were being pummeled by the waves, and enormous waves capsized the raft twice, throwing Ernie into the ocean.

Art by Keith Robinson

As the launch from the *Active* approached Ernie Hazard's tiny, inflatable raft, rescuers saw no signs of life.

QM2 Wayne A. Hennessy

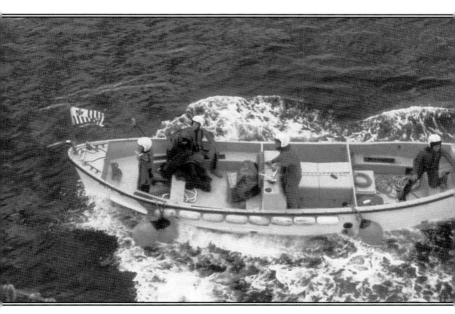

Rescuers from the Coast Guard cutter *Active* wrapped Ernie Hazard in a thick blanket; it was the first dry thing he had touched in fifty hours.

QM2 Wayne A. Hennessy

Although out of the raft and under the care of the Coast Guard, Ernie Hazard remained in peril. His skin was visibly blue, and rescuers worried that his body would go into shock.

QM2 Wayne A. Hennessy

he seemed to be propelled over a waterfall. He found himself, once more, completely submerged in the swirling water, gagging as he choked on the seawater that had caught him by surprise.

Ernie squirmed out of the bag and kicked toward the surface. Between the water and the air was a layer of foam, and he struggled, gasping, to get his head above the spume, which had the consistency of shaving cream. He swung his arms toward where he thought the raft would be, and as before, luck was with him. His hand hit the line. He grabbed it with cold fingers and slowly turned the raft until he could feel the edge of the doorway and the two-step plastic ladder, knowing that now the raft was right side up.

Aided by a kicking motion, Ernie first thrust his torso inside and then used his legs on the ladder to get the rest of his body in. More than a foot of water was sloshing on the raft's floor, and Ernie collapsed into it. He tried to find the strength to get back into the sitting position opposite the door before the next wall of water descended.

His eyes stung from the salt, and Ernie groped about the raft until he felt the survival bag, relieved it was still safely tucked inside the raft. His heart was pounding so hard, it felt like it would burst from his chest. He used what little strength he had left to pull himself up and sit with his back against the canopy wall. Hearing the next breaker roar down on him, he tensed his body, preparing for the blow. This one broke after sliding beneath the raft, and Ernie felt his rubberized capsule sail down into the trough.

Ernie's mind begged for rest, for just a snatch of sleep, but letting his guard down for even a minute could end in disaster. He had to balance the raft to keep the door in the lee of the storm, or the sea would come flooding in and bury both him and the raft. The waves were not uniform in height, which made Ernie's situation all the more challenging. Twenty waves would hit the raft in the exact same way with the exact same power, and then suddenly one would be a bit larger, a bit steeper, and break directly on him.

The battle raged on with no letup for several more agonizing hours. Ernie made it to midnight without mishap. He was halfway to dawn, halfway to what he hoped would be salvation. But the storm was not through. Sometime in the latter half of the night a breaker careened into the raft and he felt himself being lifted. The wave sent the raft over on its side. Ernie held position as best he could as he spun and tumbled in the dark void. Luckily, the raft did a complete 360-degree turn, and somehow Ernie maintained his sitting position. How many more hits could he and the raft take before one or the other came unglued?

Over and over he told himself, *Ride it out, just ride it out.* The most difficult part, though, was that he had no idea how long he would have to keep fighting. There was no finish line in sight. If he had a watch he could read in the dark, he could have marked off each hour. But without a watch, it was difficult to judge how much time remained until dawn. Nearly twenty-four hours after the freak storm began, the waves showed no signs of letting up. *Just get through this night*, thought Ernie. *I can take this. Just a little longer.*

DAWN

EASTWARD, A HINT OF PALE GRAY LIGHT FAINTLY illuminated the desolate horizon of endless ocean. It was one of the most welcome sights Ernie Hazard had ever seen. He let out a long sigh. *Maybe today.*

He had made it through more than twelve punishing hours of complete darkness. Battered and bruised, he had managed to stay inside the raft all night by constantly balancing and maintaining his sitting position while fighting off overwhelming fatigue. Now he poked his head outside the raft's canopy. He looked upon a monotonous landscape of towering gray-green hills of water streaked with white, as far as the eye could see. Fortunately, the waves had diminished in size, and the wind had calmed somewhat. The waves still had enough kick to knock the raft around, but they no longer broke under their own weight. Ernie, however, was still wary; he had come too far to let a wave sucker punch him.

The skin on his elbows and back was raw and red from chafing against the raft's fabric, and his head, neck, and back ached. His body desperately craved sleep. All he could manage, however, was a few seconds of fitful dozing before the motion of the seas again jolted him awake. Here was a new kind of torture, different from the life-or-death struggles of fighting to stay inside the raft. This was more insidious; each time he began to relax, the sudden motion of a wave jolted him from rest like a sadistic taskmaster poking him with a stick.

Ernie's ordeal was becoming as much a psychological battle as it was a physical one, but he held fast to the mindset of a survivor rather than a victim. Ernie still believed that if he was to survive, he would need to do everything he could to increase his chances of being found alive. He did not pray because he felt his best chance was to fight. He needed to keep his mind sharp and his eyes vigilant. If he made it out of this hell alive, there would be plenty of opportunity to give prayers of thanks. Right now he knew he was on his own, and only *action* was going to see him through.

Under the circumstances, Ernie's clarity of thought and his refusal to be lulled into a false sense of security were triumphs in themselves. He knew there was no guarantee that he would ever be found. Ernie's great hope now was that the men on the *Sea Fever* or *Broadbill* had become alarmed by the length of time that had gone by without a radio message from the *Fair Wind*.

Ernie had to expend valuable energy pushing cold water out the door with the small paddle. Despite the effort, he was glad for the chore—it gave him something to do and offered a brief diversion from the discomfort of the cold, which he felt down to his very core.

Now that there was a bit of light illuminating the inside of the raft, he decided to open the survival bag and extract a can of water. He had been incredibly fortunate that he'd successfully endured the night without getting seasick. That would have increased the likelihood of weakness and dehydration. Still, his thirst was great as he held a ten-ounce can of water in his shaking hand. The can did not have a flip-top and Ernie rummaged through the survival bag looking for a can opener, but all he found was a knife. The knife, however, had a blunt end rather than a point and was useless when it came to puncturing the can. Ernie saw the irony—the blunt-nosed knife was probably selected so that it wouldn't inadvertently puncture the raft, but it now left him without a tool to open the can. He brought the can to his mouth and tried to bite a hole in the top, first with his front teeth, then with his incisors. The can was too thick.

Frustrated, he turned back to the bag and began looking through it again. He saw a can opener wedged at the bottom of the bag! He quickly opened the can and greedily drank down every drop. Almost immediately he felt revived. This was his first drink of fresh water in eighteen hours, and after all the salt water he had swallowed, it tasted fantastic. There were five cans left, and he decided not to drink again until the end of the day.

Also in the bag was a can of protein cookies, and Ernie ate one, savoring each small bite. He had not eaten since Friday, and he was ravenous from expending so much energy, but like the cans of water, he didn't dare consume any more cookies. With great willpower he closed the cookie tin and placed it back in the bag. He then inspected the bellows pump for the raft's air chambers and the signal flares inside the survival bag.

There were two types of flares, several small handheld flares and a canister of cartridges. Each cartridge was slightly larger than a pencil and was equipped with a firing pin. A six-pack of flares was in the canister and each one could be screwed onto the top of the cartridge. The instructions inside the survival bag explained that the cartridge could be fired and the flare would make an arc of light approximately one hundred feet long.

The survival bag really did mean survival to Ernie. Having fresh water eliminated the overwhelming temptation some castaways have to drink seawater, which, instead of relieving thirst, increases it as well as the corresponding dehydration. Castaways, even those who know the dangers of drinking seawater, often approach the act cautiously. They tell themselves they will just take a few drops and rinse out their mouths, but they inevitably swallow a bit. Then they do it again and again, thinking that so little an amount cannot cause any harm, when in fact it will surely kill them.

The heavy sodium content of seawater must be removed by urinating. In the case of an already dehydrated person, this urination triggers the body to use up precious fluids from muscles, organs, and tissue in its effort to rid itself of sodium. It also causes brain damage by pulling moisture out of the brain cells. Delirium can set in within two hours of the initial consumption. Those who drink even a few sips of seawater without the benefit of drinking fresh water hallucinate and sometimes climb out of a raft and enter the water, thinking they are stepping onto land or toward a familiar object.

A particularly chilling account of seawater consumption was chronicled in the book *Albatross*, by Deborah Scaling Kiley and Meg Noonan. After abandoning the yacht *Trashman*, one of the shipwrecked men on the raft had consumed seawater and suddenly announced he was "going to get the car." Sharks had been circling for hours, but it didn't stop him from leaving the raft against the pleas of survivors Brad

Cavanaugh and Deb Scaling and swimming toward what he thought was his car. His fellow castaways saw his head bob up on a swell and then heard a terrible scream before he was pulled under the waves by the sharks.

As grateful as Ernie was for the contents of his survival bag, he would have benefited from a more comprehensive one that contained a blanket in a waterproof bag, a first-aid kit with painkillers, a bailer, and a sea anchor. A sea anchor, also known as a drift anchor or drogue, is a device usually made of fabric, often funnel shaped. The sea anchor is tethered to the vessel, and as the sea passes through it or is impeded by it, the drift rate of the vessel is slowed. This would have helped Ernie by keeping him closer to the last known position of the *Fair Wind*, increasing his chances of being found if a search was conducted.

Ernie estimated that the winds and seas were pushing the raft to the southeast. If that drift continued he'd soon be off Georges Bank and away from any fishing boats. Sarcastically, he thought, *Next stop, Spain*. Rescue, if it was indeed coming, had to arrive soon.

As he drifted, Ernie thought back on the accident,

wondering if there was anything he and Billy could have done differently. They had routinely monitored the weather forecasts before the storm caught them by surprise. Once in the storm's grip, they had flooded the center lobster tank for stability, secured all the gear, and turned their bow into the growing waves. No, they had taken the right precautions and had done their best.

Thinking of the actions he and Billy had taken made him mourn for his lost crewmates, and those thoughts, more than the physical punishment he was taking from the ocean, caused the first crack in Ernie's determined resolve. He thought of Dave Berry, who never even had a chance, trapped down below in the bunkroom when the *Fair Wind* pitchpoled. Dave had been a pleasure to work with. Growing up in Marblehead, he had always loved the sea, and on these trips he kept a detailed log of where and at what depth they caught lobsters during different times of the year. Both Dave and Rob Thayer were young, twenty and twenty-two respectively, and Ernie felt close to them.

Billy, thirty, was almost the same age as Ernie. Billy and Ernie had formed a close friendship, and Billy made it a point to introduce Ernie to all the important people in his life. Together they made an interesting duo. Billy was short and wiry, while Ernie was tall and brawny, and both had thick beards, Billy's reddish brown and Ernie's jet black. No one would mistake them for brothers, but they looked out for each other as brothers do.

How different it would be, thought Ernie, if his friends had escaped the *Fair Wind* and were here in the raft with him. Someone to talk to, to bolster his spirits, maybe even to joke with to relieve the tension. Sure, they would have been packed tight, their elbows, knees, and feet hitting one another. But that little bit of discomfort would have been nothing compared to the peace of mind of having the whole crew in the battle together. Instead the men's lifeless bodies were likely trapped inside the *Fair Wind* lying on the bottom of the ocean.

The thoughts about his friends sent a deep despondency through Ernie, and he knew that for now, he had to force them from his mind. To do that, he kept as busy as possible. The ribbed air chambers that held up the raft's canopy were sagging from the pounding of the seas and appeared to have lost a significant amount of air. Ernie carefully attached the bellows hand pump to a valve and pumped air into the ribbed chambers. When he removed the pump, however, an ominous hissing sound came from the valve. Air was leaking from the valve itself. Ernie's mind raced, trying to think of a way to stop it. Using the knife, he cut a patch from the survival bag and then tied the patch over the valve with line from the raft's tether. His patch seemed to stem the flow of air, but not entirely. Over the next few minutes the canopy slowly deflated to the point where it was resting on his head, and so he took out the pump and once again sent air into the ribs, and tied the valve off with the patch.

Ernie tried to doze off, thinking that if he was not rescued today, he might have to stay awake all night. He knew his chances of being found might be better in the dark when one of his flares could be seen. The constant advance of waves would not let him sleep, but he did shut his eyes and tried to conserve energy until a new hissing sound roused him into action. A valve on one of the main circular rings that kept the raft afloat was leaking. Ernie scrambled to cut another patch from his survival bag. After the patch was ready he first used the pump to add more air into the chamber and then tied the patch over the valve.

As the morning progressed, Ernie fell into a routine of pumping both the arches and the circular ring every twenty or thirty minutes. He wasn't sure his efforts were making much of a difference, but it gave him something to do. Survival experts know that keeping oneself productively occupied is crucial to maintaining the mental toughness to fight on rather than give up. Ernie instinctively knew this.

Ernie also acknowledged that the leaks were replacing the waves as his main adversary and source of concern. He wondered if there were leaks he couldn't see on the outside of the raft. No raft on the market could have survived unscathed the constant pounding of such giant seas. Ernie also realized that his decision to keep the raft tethered to the *Fair Wind* for almost an hour had certainly strained the raft further. He was prepared, however, to live with that decision. If he had to do it all over again, he'd make the same choice: to stay by the boat for as long as there remained an ounce of hope that its crew could escape.

The nearly constant pumping gave Ernie a brief diversion from the bone-chilling cold, but all he had to do was glance at his feet to know that hypothermia was taking its toll. They were numb and had turned an ugly shade of purple. He tried massaging them, but it did little good. Periodically he peered out the door, still hoping to see a boat, knowing time was running out.

Chapter 19

A SEARCH BEGINS

ERNIE WAS NOT THE ONLY ONE WHO HAD JUST EXPE-
rienced the longest night of his life in this storm.
Peter, Sarge, and Brad had remained aboard the *Sea
Fever* crouched on the port side of the deck, feet
braced against the engine block, wondering if the
next wave would end it all. The pump dropped by the
Coast Guard pilots had helped to stem the flooding.
The waves, however, still lifted the port side to pre-
carious heights. Each time the men looked down into
the void on the starboard side, they were reminded of
how little separated them from the cold and hungry sea.

For Brad, the hockey player, the pounding felt
like being checked into the boards from behind again
and again. For Peter, who had weathered plenty of

storms with his father, the intensity of this one defied description. Sarge figured the experience was not unlike being caught in a nighttime ambush, with no retreat route. The cumulative effects of each hour of terror and uncertainty were wearing down the men's fortitude, and it was a struggle to keep their primal fear at bay. They still needed to function; they might be forced to spring into action to save themselves with only a second to spare.

And so their goal throughout the night was simple: just hang on until morning. Each, however, had his doubts. At times they couldn't help but second-guess their decision not to be airlifted off the foundering boat by the helicopter. They knew that if something happened at night and they ended up in the water, Grant Moore on the *Broadbill* probably would not be able to save them. Their survival suits would keep them afloat and protected from hypothermia, but in the crazed, windswept, foam-filled seas they likely would not be found.

The mental strain gnawed at all of them. How much more, they wondered, would the *Sea Fever* be able to handle before its wooden hull opened up and water came gushing in?

In the darkness the three remaining crew of the *Sea Fever* talked little, but they were all thinking similar thoughts. "I thought of Gary over and over," says Peter. "And I thought of his wife, remembering that she was pregnant with her first child. How could I ever tell her what happened? Those hours were so long and miserable I wondered if morning would ever come." Brad was in a similar state of despair: "I was absolutely crushed thinking about Gary. I'd worked side by side with him all summer, and I couldn't bear the thought that he was gone for good."

Sarge couldn't help thinking how surreal it all felt. Just a few hours earlier he had been asleep in his bunk heading out for another routine trip, and now he was mourning his friend Gary. He remembered throwing the line so that it landed right next to Gary in the water, but Gary was so stunned he didn't move. They had done everything they could to save him and none of it worked.

Grant Moore on the *Broadbill* called Peter every half hour to check on the men and offer what little encouragement he could. Twenty miles to the east, aboard the *Sea Star*, Bob Brown, Mike Sosnowski, and the crew were now banging their way through torrential rain and house-sized waves toward the *Sea Fever*. The vessel's engine was under tremendous strain. Each time they reached the crest of a wave, the propellers came out of the sea, and when they plunged back into the water, the suddenness taxed the engine.

Fortunately, the *Sea Star* was larger than the *Sea Fever*, and Bob Brown had more than twenty years' experience riding through storms, although he would later say, "I've never seen anything like that storm, and we've been through plenty of seventy-to-eighty-mile-per-hour gales."

Knowing that the *Broadbill* was alongside Peter that night, Bob decided to veer a bit to the southwest to check on the *Fair Wind*. He was not overly concerned that he hadn't heard from the boat, but figured he'd take a quick look. He later said, "It was still pretty nasty, but when we got into the vicinity of the *Fair Wind*—where we thought her last position was— we looked for any lights, any sign of them. There was no sign, but there was still an awfully big sea going. You could be in the trough when they could be up and vice versa, so it wouldn't be unusual that you didn't see them, but we tried."

Mike Sosnowski remembers that he and Bob took

shifts on the wheel. "The seas were so bad that even if we went through a debris field we wouldn't have seen anything." Neither Mike nor Bob had any specific information about the *Fair Wind*, but in a storm like this one, every boat was vulnerable.

It was now early morning on Sunday, November 23, and using the radio they tried to raise the *Fair Wind* without success. They hoped they'd find that the *Fair Wind* had gone to the aid of the *Sea Fever*.

Back on board the *Sea Fever*, Peter kept a grim vigil, monitoring the pump, checking in with Grant, and fighting overwhelming exhaustion. It wasn't until just before dawn that he and his crew felt the waves had lost enough power to allow them to rise from their wedged position without being knocked overboard. They also knew the cutter *Active* was on its way out to them. For the first time in sixteen hours Peter, Brad, and Sarge allowed themselves to let their guard down just a bit. If the boat held together until dawn, just an hour away, they knew they would live.

Grant Moore had been so busy positioning his boat next to Peter's that he hadn't had time to think about the *Fair Wind*. But early Sunday morning he realized he had not heard from Captain Billy Garnos in quite a while. Grant repeatedly tried to raise Billy on the radio. When no response came back, he grew alarmed and decided to radio the *Fair Wind*'s owner, Charlie Raymond.

"I said, 'Charlie, we've been in a bad blow and I haven't heard from your boat. I think you better call the Coast Guard.'" (The Coast Guard does not start a search for an overdue vessel or one that is not communicating until the owner requests it.) Charlie immediately called the Coast Guard in Boston, and they in turn radioed the cutter *Active*.

The *Active* was already steaming out to Georges Bank to help Peter. Now the captain of the cutter was informed there might be a second boat in trouble. Charlie started calling the families of the men on his boat and explained the situation and that the Coast Guard had begun a search. Charlie was still hopeful, however. "At that point," recalls Charlie, "I was thinking maybe it was just a busted antenna, and everything would be okay."

Chapter 20

HEADING HOME AND ALL ALONE

TOMMY DUTTON HAD SEEN ALL KINDS OF SEA CONDI-
tions while serving aboard the Coast Guard cutter
Active, but he recalled that the nighttime mission to
assist the *Sea Fever* was particularly harsh. "It was
awful," says Dutton, "big seas, very cold, and incredible winds. Although the *Active* was 210 feet, it was a
lousy riding boat in bad weather. It really took some
bad rolls."

The *Active* arrived at the *Sea Fever* on Sunday
morning about 8:00. Seas had diminished to twenty
to twenty-five feet, and a low leaden cloud cover
added its gloom to the scene. Dutton knew that a man

had been lost overboard from the crippled vessel. The forty-seven-foot *Sea Fever* looked especially small, riding up and over the soaring pewter-colored seas. When the lobster boat was down in the troughs, it was completely hidden by the waves. The cutter made a wide circle around the *Sea Fever* to observe how the vessel was riding and to look at its damaged side.

Brad Bowen, exhausted and shaken, watched the cutter as if in a dream. "Seeing that cutter was one of the warmest things I ever experienced. We didn't really need them at that point, but it was still good to know they were on the scene…just in case."

Carl Helman, commander of the *Active*, raised Peter on the radio and asked whether he and his crew wanted to be taken off the boat. Peter responded that the worst was over and that with the *Broadbill* standing by they should be okay.

The *Broadbill* maneuvered alongside the *Sea Fever*, and plywood was handed over. Peter and his crew used it to patch up the blown windshield. Peter also roped off the blown-out side of the pilothouse. Then he put the engine in gear to see how the boat responded. It seemed to ride well enough, and Peter informed the *Active* that his father, aboard the *Sea*

Star, was due to arrive any minute and would escort him back to port. Peter also expressed his concern that no one had heard from the *Fair Wind*, and he gave his best estimate of its last known position.

Coast Guard regional headquarters in Boston had also been in touch with Helman and explained that the owner of the *Fair Wind* had requested an immediate search. Helman then became the on-scene commander for the search and rescue of the missing vessel. That gave him control over both the cutters and the aircraft that would be involved in the search. Helman, realizing the *Sea Fever* was seaworthy, immediately headed the cutter toward the last known position of the *Fair Wind*. Joining the *Active* in the search for the *Fair Wind* were an HU-16E amphibious seaplane from Air Station Cape Cod and an HC-130 airplane from Elizabeth City, North Carolina.

Active radioman Bill Gatter recalls discussing the *Fair Wind* with both Grant and Peter, trying to learn everything he could about the missing boat. "They told us the *Fair Wind* had an experienced captain and that the boat had all the latest equipment and survival gear. The problem was that no one knew exactly where the boat was at the time of their last communication. I didn't think there was a chance of finding anyone."

Not long after the *Active* plowed off to the southeast in search of the *Fair Wind*, Bob Brown and Mike Sosnowski on the *Sea Star* reached the spot where the *Sea Fever* and the *Broadbill* had been holding position. Peter and his father decided that Peter would immediately begin heading back to Hyannis and that Bob would follow a mile behind him. Peter's radar had been knocked out, so Bob would keep him on course.

Grant Moore on the *Broadbill* recalls talking to Bob when he arrived on scene. "Bob acted as if almost nothing had happened. I couldn't believe how insensitive he was to what we had all been through. But that was Bob."

With Bob on the scene, Grant decided to conduct a search for the body of Gary Brown, but quickly realized how futile his efforts were in mile after mile of twenty-foot rollers. After searching for an hour he radioed Peter and wished him a safe trip home. Grant then went back to his original location to retrieve his lobster gear. "We tried hauling gear late Sunday," says Grant, "but our hearts weren't in it, so we headed home."

As the damaged *Sea Fever* slowly headed west, Sarge, Brad, and Peter felt relief but no joy. "The mood," says Peter, "was sorrowful. There was no sense of happiness at being alive, just a hollow feeling about Gary. I kept going over what happened, wondering if we could have done anything different." In this exhausted and traumatized state of mind, the three remaining crew of the *Sea Fever* now faced an eighteen-hour trip back to Hyannis on Cape Cod.

———————————✦———————————

The specifics of the *Sea Fever*'s ordeal hit the Massachusetts newspapers Sunday morning. The following brief article ran on the front page of the Lynn *Sunday Post*:

WINDS CREATE CRISIS AT SEA, U.S. COAST GUARD RUSHING TO RESCUE

The U.S. Coast Guard embarked on several rescue missions late yesterday afternoon. One unidentified man was feared lost at sea as the Coast Guard vessel *Active* was rushing to the scene last night. The man was reportedly washed over in mountainous seas. Coast Guard spokesmen explained that a lobster boat, the *Sea Fever*, from an unknown port, with three people aboard, radioed a distress signal reporting the crewman overboard just before radio contact was lost. A fishing vessel, the *Broadbill*, was approximately two hours distant and was attempting to reach them.

Although the newspapers had not yet learned that the *Fair Wind* had been out of contact since the height of the storm, family members of the crew had begun to hear that the boat was missing. Maria Pavlis, Billy Garnos's fiancée, received a call from Billy's mother Sunday morning. "She just said I needed to come over to the house," recalls Maria. "I thought maybe something happened to Billy, but because she was so calm, I didn't expect anything really bad. When I got there, she told me that no one had been able to raise the *Fair Wind* on the radio and that Billy had not been heard from since Saturday morning. We didn't really know about the severity of the storm, so I was hoping that the boat just had trouble with its radio or maybe its engine was dead. I figured the Coast Guard would find them, or at least that's what I told myself and Billy's parents."

Dave Berry's mother, Nancy Antonich, first heard about the *Fair Wind* when her son Jeff called her and said the boat was missing. "There was nothing we could do but wait, and for me that meant pacing. The feeling of trepidation and dread was so overwhelming I just could not sit still, and I just kept walking back and forth through the house—anything to keep moving."

For friends connected to the *Fair Wind*, reports in the Sunday paper about the surprise storm were what made them first suspect the *Fair Wind* might have gotten into trouble at Georges Bank. Fishing boat captain Hugh Bishop remembers that on Saturday in Marblehead there was no indication of how bad the seas were offshore. "The first time I even realized there was a problem," says Hugh, "was Sunday morning when I was reading the *Boston Globe*. There was an article about how the Coast Guard had responded to a number of Maydays on Saturday, including one at Georges Bank. I called Bob Brown's wife, Linda, and she confirmed that the *Sea Fever* had been in trouble, but she didn't have all the details. And all she knew about the *Fair Wind* was that it hadn't been heard from in a while."

Hugh especially knew about the dangers of working offshore at Georges Bank, because he had fished the area in his fifty-foot wooden boat for several years. "In 1979 I switched to working the waters closer to shore. I figured if I had nine lives, I'd used up eight of them, and I decided that I'd had enough close calls out at Georges Bank."

There was one person who would need Hugh's luck in the coming hours, and that was Ernie, alone and drifting eastward, headed off the Bank.

Chapter 21

DRIFTING EAST

Slate-gray clouds scudded over bleak rolling swells where Ernie's orange life raft continued to ride up, then down the twenty-foot rollers. Air continued to leak from the raft, and Ernie had to pump more often to keep up with the increased outflow of air. It was now afternoon, and except for the gusting sound of the wind hitting the canopy, no noise broke the monotony. Ernie had been hoping to hear just one sound, the drone of a motor from either a plane or a fishing boat. But so far he seemed to be the only living thing left on the planet.

Beneath Ernie, however, were fish, from halibut to swordfish and the occasional shark, roaming the depths of the sea. Georges Bank, with its rich fisheries, hosted a wide array of sharks, but fortunately, by late November, the great white sharks would have moved south to warmer waters. However, blue sharks, which can grow to a length of nine feet and weigh four hundred pounds, stay out at the Bank as long as the water temperature stays above 50 degrees. On that Sunday after the storm the ocean temperature was in the low 50s.

With a slender, sleek body, the blue shark is capable of quick acceleration when it spots prey.

Life rafts have long been known to attract sharks because they represent something different to the fish: a floating object, shade from the sun, a strange color, and perhaps the splashing noise of a person bailing. Sharks come to check out the raft and then might linger to feed on the nearby fish. The blue shark in particular may be attracted by the orange coloring of a raft; tournament fishermen who go after this species know that orange is the blue's favorite color, and so they use orange lures when angling. Ernie's raft, like almost all life rafts, was a bright orange, designed to assist searchers when scanning the seas.

Blue sharks are opportunistic feeders and occasionally venture into inshore waters, putting them in contact with people. Usually the sharks investigate swimmers and waders and then glide off, with the person never knowing that an eight- or nine-foot predator has passed within a few feet. But every now and then, a blue will act differently, and there have been attacks on humans. This has happened along the Eastern Seaboard, including Cape Cod, where an aggressive blue shark once ripped into a person wading in Truro, resulting in a leg gash that required forty-six stitches.

Another species of shark that prowls the waters of Georges Bank in the fall is the mako, and this predator is even larger than the blue—in fact, makos sometimes attack and eat blues. Makos grow to twelve feet in length and 1,600 pounds. They are the fastest of all sharks, capable of incredible bursts of speed that enable them to capture and kill swordfish, tuna, porpoises, and just about any other creature in the ocean. Like the blue shark, makos have attacked humans. There have even been accounts of makos that, after having broken free of a fisherman's line, turned back and attacked the boat. Makos are related to the great white shark. One of the largest makos ever caught by man—weighing in at more than 1,500 pounds—was killed just thirteen miles off the Massachusetts coast.

Sometimes a shark will "set up shop" by a life raft, lurking just beneath it and using it as cover from which to ambush prey. The hanging ballast bag offers a temporary residence for smaller fish, which also attracts the attention of a shark. Often, sharks will bump and bang against the underside of a life raft, sometimes quite violently. The reason for this is not entirely clear, but it may be because the shark senses there is life—food—inside the raft.

Ernie, ever pragmatic, did not concern himself with thoughts of sharks. He'd seen plenty of sharks on Georges Bank and knew a few still lingered on in the fall, but he had to deal with the more immediate threat of keeping air in his raft and keeping his mind functioning despite the cold. If a plane or a ship came by and he did not use the opportunity to fire off a flare, all his past effort might be wasted.

His limbs were stiff and sore, and although he changed positions frequently, he could not find a comfortable place to sit. He tried lying on his side but quickly abandoned that position, thinking the waves were still too big to risk being so vulnerable with no means of balancing if the raft took a particularly hard hit. Lying down also meant keeping more of his body in the water because no matter how much he bailed, water was still sloshing in the raft's bottom. Besides, there was really no time to lie down as air continued to leak out the raft's valves. Ernie wasn't sure if the problem was with the valve or maybe from his own improper resealing. He had been unable to read all the directions about the raft before they were swept away in the first hour of his ordeal.

Ernie may have cursed the sea, but he never cursed the raft. This was his life capsule, and it had served him well in the face of terrific danger, and he attended to it carefully. At midafternoon he decided to repair the tattered nylon door, which had been ripped in three corners. Using the blunt-nosed knife, he cut a section of a heaving line and proceeded to stitch as well as he could, knowing every little bit of protection from the wind was important.

Although stitching the door provided a minuscule measure of achievement, Ernie's continued action was indirectly fortifying his determination to fight on. Fixing things such as the door and putting patches over the valves was second nature to Ernie. He was able to quickly size up a problem and then get to work.

From past experience, he also knew about surviving

close calls and the importance of luck. In fact, Ernie had been lucky in this sense all his life. When he was ten years old, he was biking and didn't see the car speeding directly toward him. He was struck on the leg and sent careening through the air. He was knocked unconscious and didn't come to until he was in an ambulance. Amazingly, he survived with nothing more than a broken leg and a few bruises and scrapes.

His string of close calls and good fortune continued. When he was twelve years old, on a cold winter's day, he was ice fishing alone when the ice gave way. The depth was over his head, and no matter how hard he tried to hoist himself out of the freezing water, he could not maintain a grip on the slippery ice. Luckily he wasn't too far from shore and was able to grab the tip of a tree branch. Slowly, hand over hand, he secured a firm grip on the thicker part of the branch. Then he was able to hoist his torso up on the ice, followed by his legs. He then walked home.

But perhaps his closest brush with death happened when he was twenty-five and riding his motorcycle. A driver of an automobile ran a stop sign on a side road just as Ernie was cruising by on the main road. The front wheel of Ernie's motorcycle hit the side of the car. The impact stopped the motorcycle dead in its tracks, but the forward momentum sent Ernie flying up and over the car. He landed in the center of the main road. Stunned, Ernie slowly got to his feet, amazed that he seemed to be in one piece with nothing broken. Had the car run the stop sign just a split second later, Ernie would have been hit broadside and the outcome would have been very different.

And now, shaking with cold inside the raft, he knew he needed another stroke of luck or the raft would become his coffin. The afternoon was waning, and Ernie knew that the air temperature of about 45 degrees would drop during the night. He had now been either wet or in the water for more than twenty-four hours. His core temperature likely had dropped, perhaps to as low as 94 degrees, and the chill continued its inexorable march from his extremities toward his torso. With each passing hour his blood thickened and slowed while his capillaries constricted. This caused his feet to become swollen, purple lumps. The cold had become a part of his very being, as if he'd never been warm, and he fantasized about a hot shower.

Adding to his discomfort, only a single layer of fabric separated him from the ocean, and the cold water beneath him was sucking away his body heat. (Today's rafts are outfitted with an air chamber on the floor for insulation against the sea. Back in 1980, however, most had only a bare uninsulated floor.) He tried to keep his mind on his tasks of bailing and pumping, but his thoughts kept returning to the fact that he had not heard a single search plane or helicopter the entire day.

As the raft rode the waves to the east, Ernie thought, *I'm heading in the wrong direction. If anyone is looking for me they better search this edge of the Bank.* He tried to calculate how far he might have drifted from the *Fair Wind*'s last location. He estimated his drift to be between twenty and sixty miles. Ernie had no real way of knowing if he was even still on Georges Bank.

Despite suffering from the cold and a terrible ache throughout most of his body, Ernie was in far better shape than most victims in similar situations. The extreme cold had not yet affected his judgment. Hypothermia eventually renders the thinking process disjointed and sluggish because the slow-circulating blood doesn't bring the brain enough oxygen. Should Ernie have fallen into a state of confusion and indifference, he would likely not have continued his pumping schedule, and the raft might have completely collapsed.

———◆———

The pale light coming through the clouds began diminishing as evening closed in on Ernie and the raft. A part of his brain relived the accident over and over, and Ernie battled to keep those thoughts from taking over. *Keep busy*, he told himself, *just keep bailing and pumping. Forget about what happened.* His mood had been relatively steady up to this point, and he knew instinctively that should it start careening between highs and lows, he might not recover from one of the lows.

His mind struggled back and forth between dealing with what he could control and thinking about rescue and what-ifs. *What if no one knows the boat sank?... What if I go another day, another two?*

Without having to fight the waves, he had too much time to think, and a particularly terrible thought now bubbled up. Was the *Sea Fever* okay? It had been the closest boat to the *Fair Wind*, the one Billy had been talking with on the radio at the beginning of the storm. Theirs would be the first boat crew to wonder why they hadn't heard from the *Fair Wind*. But if the *Sea Fever* had gone down, maybe no one else thought of the *Fair Wind*.

He tried pushing these what-ifs out of his mind, but they kept coming. *What if the* Sea Fever *crew are in a life raft just like me and time's running out for them… or what if they went down so quick they couldn't get out? The same monstrous wave that capsized our boat could have done the same to them.* Ernie considered the bleak possibility that if the captains of the *Sea Fever* and the *Fair Wind* had spoken only to each other and if both boats were gone, no other vessel would miss either one immediately. He tried to recall if Bob Brown on the *Sea Star* had been working the Bank, but he just couldn't remember.

Ernie was starting to feel sorry for himself, and to change his focus he directed his thoughts away from rescuers and back to his raft. *What do I have to do to survive another day, another two days, or more?* he asked himself. *I'm going to pull this off. I didn't spend all this time fighting just to give up now.* Ernie simply refused to accept that everything he had done thus far would lead only to a slow death, a fate worse than the one suffered by his crewmates.

Chapter 22

THE SEARCH

PLOWING THROUGH TWENTY-FOOT SWELLS, THE COAST Guard cutter *Active* arrived at the *Fair Wind*'s last known position by midafternoon on Sunday. Tommy Dutton stood out on the deck with binoculars in hand and scanned the seas for colors and shapes other than the gray ocean. He was searching not only for the boat itself but for anything that might catch his eye: bait buckets, barrels, a life raft, an orange survival suit, a life jacket, or a body. But nothing interrupted the dark rollers.

"I didn't have much hope of us finding anything," says Dutton, "particularly not someone alive because I knew what the conditions were like the day before."

The *Active*'s radioman, Bill Gatter, and Quartermaster Second Class Wayne Hennessy agreed. "I didn't think there was a chance of us finding anyone, or even any debris, because the search area was so large," says Gatter. Hennessy was hoping they'd get lucky and find the *Fair Wind* still afloat because "if it wasn't, we doubted anyone would be found alive in late November."

The Boston operations center gave the cutter a search area to concentrate on based on the estimated drift of the *Fair Wind* with winds and currents. "In addition," recalls Operations Officer Dave Nicholson, "we decided to drop our own data buoy to try and get another sense of the drift. Our data buoy indicated the search should extend a little farther to the east, so we started expanding our hunt beyond the initial area."

The overall search area, however, was enormous, covering five thousand square miles, and aircraft launched from both Cape Cod and Elizabeth City, North Carolina, probably had a better chance than the *Active* of spotting any sign of the *Fair Wind* or its crew. This search would be harder than looking for the proverbial needle in the haystack; it was like looking for a needle in an entire field of hay.

As evening approached, the men on board the

Active were growing more disheartened about the chances that the *Fair Wind* was still afloat. The Coast Guard men now felt they were no longer conducting a search and rescue mission, but merely a search. Some figured that since the current search was for a lost cause, they might as well steam back to land to be home in time for Thanksgiving. The *Fair Wind*, they thought, had sunk and disappeared forever.

When boats the size of the *Fair Wind* disappear without issuing a radio Mayday, the cause of the accident is never known. On-board fire, explosion, capsizing, blown hatch covers, smashed windshields, cracked hulls, or a myriad of other events can sink a boat, but when the crew doesn't even have time to radio a distress call, another incident should be investigated: collision.

Large ships run over small boats probably much more often than Coast Guard statistics suggest. The smaller boat often ends up on the bottom of the sea, and there is no way for authorities ever to determine the exact cause of the disappearance. The crew on the larger vessel either never knows they hit the boat or they know exactly what happened but refuse to stop. Every now and then, however, a crew member from the sinking vessel escapes and lives to tell what really happened.

———◆———

Sunday night brought an eerie silence as the wind all but ceased. Ernie Hazard strained to hear what he hoped would be the drone of an airplane engine coming out of the coal-black sky. He was talking to himself, debating the merits of forcing himself to stay awake or trying to get some much-needed sleep. On the one hand, he wanted to be ready to fire off a flare should he hear or see a plane or a ship, but on the other hand, his unbearable weariness was making each minute feel like an hour. Sleep deprivation had replaced the pain and discomfort of the cold as his number one misery.

To keep his spirits and his strength up, he had eaten another cookie and drunk another can of water just before the sun set. He had four cans of water and a few cookies left. Ernie had no idea how long he would need to make them last, but he was determined to stretch them out as long as he could.

Now the darkness heightened his sense of lone- liness. He craved the company of another human being, the sound of another voice. The feeling of isolation was intense, but for Ernie not as debilitating as it might have been for someone who had never truly spent time alone. Some people go through entire lives avoiding occasions where they are alone, but not Ernie. He had often enjoyed being alone and independent. Of all his life experiences, none prepared him for his current predicament better than his solitary bike ride from the state of Washington to Mexico.

Ernie came up with the idea for the journey when he was twenty-five years old, and instead of just talking about it, he had the nerve to do it. He quit his job, hitchhiked to Seattle, purchased a bicycle, and began heading south. When he began the trip, he didn't really have a goal in mind, but thought it would be nice if he could keep riding until he reached Mexico. Very little planning went into the several-week trip because he felt he could learn as he went along. He had only a few dollars in his pocket, and little more than some clothing, a tent, and a sleeping bag in his bike's saddlebags.

Ernie never knew where he would spend the night, but somehow he always found a campground or met people who invited him to stay at their house or camp in their yard. The trip was an eye-opener for Ernie in that it helped forge his growing belief that he could adapt to most any situation, and do so with little help from others. He loved the fact that each day offered something new, something different. When problems occurred, he tended to view them as minor challenges that came with the territory. Resolving those challenges added to his sense of well-being.

And so now, alone in the raft, he was not terrified by his isolation. Still, he couldn't control all his thoughts, and he remembered the dinner with his crewmates at the Backside Saloon. *Was it really just a few days ago?* he wondered. It could have been a lifetime ago. Thinking of the dinner caused him anguish, knowing everything was gone: his three friends, the *Fair Wind*, his prior life. To push such thoughts away, he turned to the repetitive chores of bailing and pumping. The tasks not only kept him busy, but they were necessary. The simple results of more air in the raft and less water in its bottom were positive outcomes, and that was exactly what his psyche needed.

Not once did Ernie try to ignore his situation or deny his new reality. He knew the odds were against him. He also knew any number of events, from a major leak to a new storm, could end his life within hours. But when he started to dwell on such things, the steely voice inside him would speak up. *Come on, Hazard, keep it going. Don't go soft now. Roll with the punches, keep doing what you're doing.*

From the beginning he accepted what had happened. There is a fine line between acceptance and resignation. He simply kept an open mind and was honest with himself that he had no idea of the final outcome, telling himself that he had done—and would continue to do—the things that would help his odds.

Still, no human can work and function without sleep, and he finally allowed himself to nap. The seas had dropped to fifteen feet. The raft rode the long swells easily, without the pitching and plunging motion of that morning. His sleep was fitful, more an intermittent doze than the restorative deep sleep that his body so desperately needed. He would doze for thirty minutes at most, and that would only bring him through the first two of the five stages of normal sleep. The sleep deprivation wasn't just depleting Ernie's energy; sooner or later it would slow his ability to react to change, make quick and logical decisions, and perform tasks.

Chapter 23

ALMOST OUT OF TIME

AT THE COAST GUARD OPERATIONS CENTER IN Boston Lieutenant Robert Eccles had not given up on finding the men of the *Fair Wind*. Eccles and fellow staff members had decided that they needed additional assistance besides the two Coast Guard airplanes already searching Georges Bank. Eccles knew that if there were survivors in a life raft, they were near the end of what they could endure of the cold, if they hadn't expired already.

Eccles called the US Naval Air Station in Brunswick, Maine, and explained the situation. It was agreed that at dawn on Monday morning, an enormous P-3 long-range patrol plane, with a crew of eleven, would set out for Georges Bank. The P-3 Orion is a four-engine turboprop aircraft built to detect submarines using electronic scanning equipment. The plane's reconnaissance capacity would be an advantage in searching for the *Fair Wind*, but because the plane was designed to locate submarines with electronics, it wasn't the best aircraft from which to visually look for a life raft. Unlike the Coast Guard HC-130, which has large windows for searches to scan the ocean below, the P-3 had limited visibility. Personnel manning the Boston Coast Guard command center knew this, but they had to use whatever resources they could, as time was running out for any survivors.

For Ernie, time stretched as endlessly as the ocean surrounding him. It was the hour just before dawn, the hour some say is the darkest of the night. Attaching the pump to the valves was difficult in the blackness, but Ernie had performed the task so many times he could do it by touch alone. Now, however, his frozen limbs felt sluggish, and for the first time his numbed hands gave him difficulty. His thickened blood labored to reach his extremities. The task of pumping the raft took a bit longer each time he performed it.

His feet were now mere raw lumps of flesh. Ernie tried to remember what it felt like to be warm, without the terrible aches. He rubbed and massaged his feet, but he wasn't sure if that was what a person should do for frostbite. He shook his head, tugged on his beard, and tried to recall the proper treatment for frozen limbs. The treatment, he told himself with a pained smile, is to get warm. The treatment is to get your butt out of this raft, get dry, and get off the ocean!

He couldn't see his feet in the dark, but he knew they were in bad shape. They were so waterlogged that when he rubbed them, it almost felt as if the skin would come off. He barely had any sensation at all from his ankles to his toes. He wondered if he'd ever get it back, if he'd ever be able to walk again. When the word *amputation* popped into his mind, he shook his head and, with a grunt, got to his knees and crawled toward the raft's opening. Sticking his head outside, he could not discern the horizon, but up above he saw a few stars in various patches. The cloud cover was breaking, and the day ahead held the promise of sun.

He thought back to the day before the accident, Friday, and remembered the sunset he had watched from the pilothouse with Billy, Rob, and Dave. *How many days ago was that? What day is today?* It took him a minute to realize that it was Monday and that the *Fair Wind* went down on Saturday, just two days ago. *Could it really have been only two days ago?* It seemed to Ernie that time had been altered in a strange way.

A common response to a disastrous accident is to relive the initial ordeal. Ernie couldn't help but think back to Saturday morning and how he was asleep in his warm bunk without the slightest advance warning that hurricane-force winds were about to assault the fishing grounds. He remembered it was about this same hour of day, just before dawn, that he climbed into the pilothouse and listened to Billy say it looked like a big blow was coming because it was getting worse by the minute. And he bitterly thought of the weather forecast he heard at that hour and how the seas were already double what the meteorologists predicted.

It was as if the weather report was backward: instead of forecasting what might be expected, it was giving conditions that had occurred three hours earlier. Again, Ernie tried to turn his mind away from what went wrong—it was just too debilitating to think his friends had died because of a faulty weather forecast.

Fortunately, Ernie had not fallen into the trap of blaming himself for what happened, as many survivors unreasonably do. Throughout history, survivors of major catastrophes rack their minds and second-guess every little decision they made. They think that if they had just done one thing differently, the whole accident could have been averted. Over and over they go through each second, each reaction, as the calamity occurred. They begin to attribute outcomes to their own action or inaction. In hindsight they see how they might have made better decisions that might have averted the accident. And so they reproach themselves, adding depression and guilt to the trauma they are already dealing with. In some cases this is the tipping point in their struggle to endure, and they slip into apathy.

Of course, apathy could still arise within Ernie simply because the sea and the cold were wearing him down. Fatigue, hypothermia, sleep deprivation, and hunger were just some of the stresses grinding away at his physical and mental health. He had been looking at his situation logically and realistically. He knew from the start, from the moment he forced himself to swim downward to get out of the flooded pilothouse, that he had been presented with a series of choices. Even now, with his mind growing listless, he knew the choice was still there: he could keep willing himself to endure more or, just as easily, will himself to die as quickly as possible. And there was the third option, the easiest of all, which was to be indifferent to his fate.

Ernie dozed for a few minutes, until his internal clock forced him awake to pump air into the raft again. He noticed that beyond the nylon canopy there was just enough gray light for him to look through a crack in the door and see the ocean sliding beneath the raft. It was clear which direction the sun would emerge from and that was the direction he was drifting, ever eastward, off the Bank.

He stuck his head out the door. Gone were the sharp edges of the waves, replaced by smooth, gently rolling swells. Instead of mountainous, jagged peaks, these waves looked like rounded foothills, and the sea a monotonous undulating void. Ernie may not have known it, but sensory deprivation was conspiring with the cold to further wear him down. There was nothing to divert him from his misery and pain, not even a breath of wind to ruffle the ocean, and every ten-foot roller was the same as the next. Twenty-four hours earlier Ernie was in sensory overload, tumbling in mountainous waves and assaulted by shrieking winds, whereas now all was calm and quiet.

Ernie was struck by his utter insignificance on this endless ocean plain, and he felt like an ant clinging to a scrap of vegetation, adrift on the indifferent sea. *How will a search plane ever spot me?* he wondered. *Everything has to go my way: a plane must fly close enough that I can hear it and then I've got to fire off a flare within a second or two.* He made sure the flares were easily accessible inside the survival bag, and he kept the bag unzipped. Should a plane pass overhead while Ernie was dozing or if he didn't fire off a flare in time, the plane would continue on and maybe never cover this part of the search grid again.

If Ernie drifted off the Bank and had the incredible long-shot odds of being in the path of a freighter or tanker, chances were the ship's crew would never notice him. In fact, he had better odds of being run down by a ship since so many ships no longer post a lookout but instead rely entirely on radar to alert them to other vessels. Many castaways who have survived long ordeals on the open sea report that ships passed within less than a hundred feet and never stopped, despite the screams of the castaways and even the shooting of flares. The castaway looks at the huge deck gliding by, hoping to see another human standing there. Instead it's as if no one is aboard the ship and it's being controlled remotely from a thousand miles away. The castaway's frustration and bitterness at intersecting the path of a ship—in thousands of miles of empty ocean—and still not being seen is sometimes more than he or she can bear.

Ernie wondered when the sun would be strong enough to break through the low, thin clouds. He hoped that its rays would provide a bit of warmth inside his domed raft, which felt more and more like a stainless-steel walk-in refrigerator. His mind wandered to creature comforts, imagining the taste of hot coffee and the way it would spread its heat into his stomach and drive out the cold. He pictured lying down in a dry bed, with layers and layers of blankets surrounding him. And when he thought of his mother and brothers, it all became too much, and he turned his attention back to pumping air into the raft.

When the pumping was finished, he looked outside again. A weak bit of sunlight filtered through the cloud cover to the east. And then he spotted the first form of life he'd seen since his ordeal began. A shearwater, an oceanic bird that spends almost its entire life at sea, flew by the raft.

The bird flew from west to east, the same direction Ernie was drifting. Through the years, Ernie had seen plenty of shearwaters and other pelagic birds out at Georges Bank, and he knew many of these birds had never even seen a human, a boat, or anything man-made. He hoped this bird would be different, that it would see not just a life raft, but a Coast Guard cutter. He knew time was running out.

Chapter 24

AT THE EDGE
OF THE BANK

As THE *SEA FEVER* APPROACHED THE DOCK IN
Hyannis, all Peter could think of was getting off the
boat. The meticulously maintained vessel that had
set out to sea just four days earlier was now a mess,
with debris strewn about below. Water still sloshed
in the bilge, and the shattered starboard side of the
pilothouse was a sorrowful reminder of where Gary
had been hurled from the boat. For the past few hours
Peter had been thinking of Gary. He pictured the
barrel-chested, redheaded Irishman on the wheel
during the storm, his left hand with a white-knuckle
grip on the wheel and his right hand on the throttle.

Then the wave hit, the boat tipped ninety degrees, and Gary was swept away. But Peter had one last look at Gary, when he was behind the boat, face up in the water with a glassy-eyed stare, looking at nothing. Yes, Peter, the distraught twenty-three-year-old captain, wanted to run from this death trap of a boat as soon as it touched the dock.

Peter knew, however, that leaving the boat immediately might not be an option because his father was right behind him in the *Sea Star*. He thought his father might insist they clean up the mess below. Surprisingly, though, when they got the boat tied up, Bob let them leave. Peter embraced his wife, and Brad, his parents. Neither man said much, totally overcome by the reunion with loved ones. "To this day," says Brad, "it's still too overwhelming to describe what it was like to see my parents standing there."

"The only thing I remember Brad saying," recalls his father, "was that the storm came out of nowhere, and he kept wondering how the weather service could have missed the forecast so badly."

Sarge had no one waiting for him; he had specifically asked the Coast Guard not to call his mother because she was ill from cancer. Instead he talked to the crew on the *Sea Star* and to Frank Collins, who owned a wholesale lobster company. Earlier Frank had received a radio message from Bob Brown, who told him when they would arrive as well as what happened to the *Sea Fever* and how nobody had heard from the *Fair Wind*. "Bob made it clear," says Frank, "that he wanted things low-key, and to make sure there was no press at the dock." Frank didn't tell anyone about what had happened because he did not want the media swarming the shell-shocked crew of the *Sea Fever*. If word got out, TV reporters would be lying in wait, hoping to get the tears on film.

Frank remembers he took one look at Peter getting off the boat and could tell what an awful toll the accident had taken. "He looked like he'd been hit with a baseball bat, almost in shock. He was a good captain and losing a man was really hard on him. Bob, on the other hand, was unemotional. He never let his feelings show. He was thinking more about how he had to get the *Sea Fever* repaired than about what happened."

And the *Sea Fever* would need extensive repairs. Besides the damage to the wheelhouse and the interior of the boat, the wooden hull had twelve cracked ribs.

"When I found out how many ribs were cracked," says Sarge, "I really thought it was a miracle that the boat had stayed afloat for as long as it did."

Sarge remembered his "storm promise" to visit his church immediately if he made it home alive. "I drove one of Bob's trucks, along with some of the crew from the *Sea Star*, back up to Marblehead, where I'd left my car at Bob's house, then I drove on to Danvers. The first thing I did was walk to church. As I was walking, somebody driving by pulled up alongside me and just stared at me like he saw a ghost. Then he shouted, 'Sarge! It's you—everybody up here thinks you drowned.' When I got to church, I just sat there and thought about things and said, 'Thank you for my life.' "

Peter's day wasn't over yet because he and his father had to go straight to the Boston Coast Guard command center and explain what happened. And so the two men climbed into Peter's truck and began the two-hour ride to Boston, saying very little. Like Ernie, Peter had gotten almost no sleep since he was awakened early Saturday morning more than two days ago.

Meanwhile, approximately two hundred miles out at sea, Ernie knew that the raft was leaking air at an ever-increasing pace. He moved from one valve to another, pumping the raft, with almost no time to rest in between. There was no longer much sense in rationing the cans of water because for the first time he felt that soon he would not be able to keep up with the leaks and the raft would sink. Then the ocean would make quick work of him.

He drank a can of water, stuck his head out of the raft and searched the lonely horizon, then went back inside and began the pumping process. The salty seawater ate into the abrasions that crisscrossed his body. Sitting was agony, but lying down was worse. He tried to stretch his legs to stop the cramping, but moving his legs was becoming harder and harder. Part of his mind told him he was probably finished, that all his effort was for nothing. But the other part, almost a voice, reminded him to keep going, that today could be the day.

A phrase from his days in the military popped into Ernie's head: "maximum use of available resources." He had stitched the door, tied patches over the valves, and controlled his intake of water and cookies. Now he turned his mind to rescue. He figured that besides the flares he needed some other movement to attract the attention of pilots, and decided he'd wave the orange survival bag outside the raft's door if a plane came. The sun had not broken through the cloud cover as Ernie had hoped, but the clouds appeared to be high up and a plane could fly below them. *They gotta come today*, he thought. *I've done all I can.*

———————

The men in the P-3 craned their necks and scanned mile after mile of gray, rolling sea. This search was very different from their submarine patrols because they couldn't rely on any of their electronics except radar, which could find a boat but not a raft. If someone was in a life raft, the radar wouldn't pick it up. The men wondered if they could spot a raft with the naked eye in such a huge expanse of ocean.

They had been flying the search grids for over an hour when radioman Craig Martin shouted that he saw something, something orange. The pilot banked the aircraft in the direction Martin pointed.

———————

Ernie was close to what can only be described as a catatonic state. It was 9:00 a.m., and hypothermia had advanced to the point where he was somewhere between life and death, enduring each minute as it came. His entire body, not just his feet, was slowly going numb.

Far off, he thought he heard a droning sound, and it took a couple of seconds for the sound's meaning to register in his brain. *A plane!*

A jolt of adrenaline coursed through his frozen limbs, and he grabbed a flare, stuck it out the door, and fired. The red flare and trailing smoke arced high into the sky. He could see the plane off in the west. He forced his shaking, half-numb hands to clutch another flare and fired it off. The plane began a turn. Now it was heading in his direction. He thrust the survival bag out the door and waved frantically. The plane roared directly over him. Finally, Ernie's three long days of uncertainty had come to an end: he knew he had been seen.

Minutes later a second, smaller plane flew over Ernie and dropped a string of orange marker buoys and a radio. The radio fell too far from the raft for him to retrieve it, but one of the marker buoys drifted by the raft's door and Ernie grabbed it. Inside was a message: "If other crewmen aboard, wave." Ernie did not wave.

The message only confirmed what Ernie had known all along, that his crewmates never got out of the *Fair Wind*. Ernie sat back. There was relief, but no jubilation at being found.

The P-3 radioed back to Boston Coast Guard command headquarters that they had spotted a raft and that someone had waved an orange bag out the door. Bob Eccles was astounded. "Even though this is exactly what I'd been hoping for, I could hardly believe it. For a P-3 to spot a tiny life raft was just about miraculous."

Eccles and the command center crew immediately notified the other planes involved in the search. They also contacted the cutter *Active*, which had been searching since it went to the aid of the *Sea Fever*. The *Active* was approximately three hours away from the raft, but it was the closest Coast Guard vessel to it.

The cutter immediately headed to the location where the raft was spotted, approximately thirty miles east of where the *Fair Wind* went down. The radioman on the *Active* was able to raise a Japanese long-liner fishing vessel that was closer to the raft and requested that it too steam toward the raft.

Family members were alerted that a raft with a person on board had been spotted and that the *Active* would be on the scene in three hours. Maria Pavlis, Billy Garnos's fiancée, remembers the roller coaster of emotions. Her hopes soared, knowing the life raft on the *Fair Wind* could hold all four crew members. The press also learned about the sighting of the raft, and area newspapers, radio, and television began reporting and speculating about who might be inside.

About noon, Ernie looked out of the raft and saw a fishing vessel, about one hundred feet in length, approaching his raft. It was the Japanese long-liner, and when it was about two hundred yards from Ernie, it stopped and stood by. Ernie wondered why the vessel halted and no one came to get him. He waited several minutes, then waved the survival bag out the door to make sure they knew someone was alive inside. The boat still did not move. For a moment Ernie wondered if his hold on reality was faltering. He wasn't imagining this boat, and those on board clearly knew he was in the raft, but why weren't they coming?

Ernie didn't know that the Coast Guard had asked the fishing vessel to stand by but not attempt a rescue because the *Active* was on the way. The Coast Guard didn't want to take any chances now, as the Japanese ship did not have a small boat to launch nor was it clear if any medical personnel were aboard the fishing boat.

After forty-eight hours in the raft, Ernie knew he could hang on awhile longer. Even in his frozen stupor it was clear the fishing boat was not going to come any closer, so Ernie figured a Coast Guard helicopter or cutter would arrive soon. He sat back inside his floating igloo, continued to pump the air chambers, and dreamed about sleeping in a warm bed.

He waited for an entire hour until he heard the sounds of another ship. This time when he looked out, he saw the white hull and the red diagonal stripe of the cutter *Active*. Help was just minutes away.

Chapter 25

SALVATION

THE FIRST STREAKS OF BLUE APPEARED BETWEEN THE cracks of the breaking cloud cover as men aboard the *Active* trained their binoculars on an orange speck off their starboard side. The Givens life raft bobbed easily on the swells, but even with the aid of binoculars the Coasties saw no signs of life on it. Wayne Hennessy began to think the P-3 pilots had been mistaken about having spotted a flare or one or more survivors because no one from the raft now waved or poked a head out the door. Tommy Dutton assumed it would be all or nothing: either all four men from the *Fair Wind* would be inside or nobody would be inside, and it was beginning to look like nobody.

Meanwhile, four young Coasties, including Tom

McKenzie, readied the *Active*'s twenty-six-foot launch. With a white hull and beige interior, the open motor-boat looked similar to a dory, except it had a steering wheel in the middle toward the port side. Once the boat was lowered into the water and the cables were unfastened, McKenzie stood at the wheel, started the motor, and sped off toward the orange speck in the distance.

"The surface of the sea was calm," says McKenzie, "but there were large rolling swells, spaced well apart at two-hundred-foot intervals. We were pretty anxious as we approached the raft because we didn't know what we'd find. Would the raft be empty or would all four crew members from the *Fair Wind* be inside? We also worried we might find them all dead."

McKenzie and crew were dressed in orange survival suits and their heads were protected by white helmets. As the launch pulled within forty feet of the raft, there was still no sign of life inside, and McKenzie began to think the worst. When the launch was just a boat length away, McKenzie was startled by an incredible sight: the raft door parted and a head appeared. *"Oh my God,"* he whispered.

"I'll never forget that moment," recalls McKenzie,

"because his skin was blue. His chest was blue, his arms were blue, and his face and neck were blue."

The men with binoculars on the cutter watched in amazement. They too could see the blue face and bare blue chest of the man in the raft. Dave Nicholson recalls thinking that if the *Active* hadn't arrived exactly when it did, the man would have been dead within a couple of hours.

McKenzie eased the small boat a bit closer to the raft. "Beneath this big bushy beard I saw this man smile. I simply could not believe he could smile after what he must have endured. I shouted to him, 'You're going to be okay now, you've made it!'"

McKenzie's side of the boat was abreast the raft, and McKenzie reached out and held the raft while the other three crew members carefully pulled Ernie into their boat. As they wrapped him in several layers of brown blankets, McKenzie asked, "You're from the *Fair Wind*?" After Ernie nodded, McKenzie asked a second question. "Could anyone else from your boat still be alive?" Ernie shook his head.

The crew sat the lone survivor down on the forward bench. One crew member sat next to him, keeping his arm around Ernie's shoulder to make sure he didn't fall over. Then McKenzie turned the boat and raced back to the *Active*, hoping to get his passenger to a medical corpsman as quickly as possible.

Ernie felt like he might collapse as he sat freezing in the blankets. Sleep, not warmth, had become his greatest need, and he let his head drop so that his chin rested on the blankets covering his chest. It was now approximately 1:00 p.m., and the wool blankets were the first dry material he had felt in almost fifty hours.

As the launch pulled alongside the *Active*, McKenzie stood at the wheel, another man stood at the bow, and a third stood ready at the stern. The crew then lowered orange bumper balls over the side of the launch next to the cutter. Ernie sat unmoving, huddled in the bow, where the fourth crew member kept a protective arm around him, telling him everything was going to be all right.

The men on the cutter lowered a line, which the boat men hooked to their bow. Now the launch was being towed alongside the *Active* at the exact same speed. McKenzie kept his hands on the wheel to keep the launch a few feet from the ship. Ernie never looked up at the ship. His whole body felt entombed in ice. And now that he was saved, exhaustion swept over him. All he could think about was a dry bed and sleeping for days.

Two large "boat falls" were lowered from the *Active*, and McKenzie's crew tied one forward and one aft. Then the skipper brought the launch in tight against the ship. As the crew of the *Active* began hoisting the launch up to the main deck, helping hands reached out from the ship for the blue man with the black beard.

Ernie raised his head a bit and mustered enough energy to slide along the bench toward the ship. Then he extended both arms. Two crew members from the launch stood in the boat and supported Ernie as he forced himself to stand for the first time since the pitchpoling. The two men in the launch and three on the cutter assisted Ernie as he stepped over the cutter's rail and onto the main deck. McKenzie then had the launch lowered again and raced off to retrieve the raft so it could be analyzed and so no other search planes or vessels would mistake it for a second life raft.

One of the blankets covering Ernie parted and the crew could see he didn't have even a T-shirt on. Wayne Hennessy remembers that the castaway looked like a mass of blue and reddish flesh that could barely move. "He was in bad shape, and I really felt for him. He was covered in abrasions, and his lips were a dark purple." Radioman Bill Gatter concurs, adding, "It was nothing short of a miracle he was alive. His flesh was blue, his joints were swollen, and he really couldn't walk."

A stretcher was waiting, and the medical corpsman— who had training similar to that of an emergency medical technician—immediately had Ernie lie down. He knew the survivor was not yet out of the woods. Ernie could still go into shock because of poor blood circulation, and the medical corpsman wanted him in a prone position to keep his blood pressure up. Ernie was susceptible to a heart attack until his core temperature returned to normal.

Any extra movement by Ernie could lead to a quick death because the sudden circulation could bring the cold blood from the outer limbs rushing toward the heart, stopping it—literally—cold. This was a critical point for a hypothermic victim, but Ernie felt nothing but relief to be away from the perpetual rocking motion of the raft and among fellow human beings who genuinely cared about his safety.

The corpsman and crew carefully lifted the stretcher and carried Ernie to the officers' room. They helped him slowly change into dry clothes, rewrapped him in blankets, and the corpsman took his vital signs. Then he placed a small bowl of soup before Ernie.

Although Ernie had eaten cookies and drunk water on the raft, the soup was beyond description, not because of its taste but because of its warmth. He savored each mouthful, as a good number of the ship's crew silently watched. It was as if they were witnessing a man rise from the dead, and they didn't want to miss a single moment. When Ernie finished the soup, Dave Nicholson debriefed him and asked about the possibility of the rest of the crew being alive.

"I remember thinking," says Nicholson, "here's this guy who has just gone through something absolutely terrible, and now I'm going to start asking him questions. But I had to know if the others from his boat had the potential to be alive. When I started talking to him, I was amazed at how coherent he was. He made it clear to us that he stayed with the overturned hull for at least forty-five minutes until it started to sink, and no one else got out. I asked him if the other crew members had survival suits on, and he answered, 'No time. It all happened so quickly. It was just luck I got out.' "

Meanwhile, Tom McKenzie had returned to the ship with the life raft in tow. McKenzie went inside to see how Ernie was doing, but Ernie was already asleep in an officer's bed. The corpsman remained worried. Ernie's feet appeared to be frostbitten and swollen to almost twice their normal size, and he was still concerned about shock or a heart attack and the limited medical facilities aboard the cutter.

The corpsman consulted with Captain Helman and recommended Ernie be airlifted off the boat and flown directly to a hospital. The captain agreed and radioed the Boston operations center to request a helicopter, then started steaming west. They let Ernie sleep.

———————◆———————

Word spread among the fishing community that one crew member of the *Fair Wind* had been found alive, but his name had not yet been released. Wholesale lobsterman Frank Collins remembers thinking, *I'll bet it's Ernie*. "I'd gotten to know Ernie," recalls Frank, "the same as I would any deckhand on a boat we unloaded, because the process took three or four hours. Ernie struck me as the kind of person who would be thinking, *How am I going to get out of this predicament*, rather than being in shock from what happened. He just seemed to have this mental toughness about him."

SEA FEVER
MARBLEHEAD

Chapter 26

THE AIRLIFT

PILOTS BUCK BALEY AND JOE TOUZIN WERE ONCE again at the controls of their HH-3F helicopter. The last four days had been grueling between the many Maydays on Saturday and the flight to the *Sea Fever* on Saturday night, and the search for the *Fair Wind* on the eastern end of Georges Bank on Sunday. Now, on Monday afternoon, they were headed back out to the Bank, only this time it was to pick up survivor Ernie Hazard.

Baley remembers thinking how incredible it was that Ernie had been found alive. "We used some very specific charts and calculations to plan, conduct, and evaluate the success of searches. The probability of detection, POD, is one calculation that helps us determine how effective a search is. Given the conditions we had been searching for Mr. Hazard in, I figured we had about a 6 percent chance of finding him, and that assumed we were looking in an area where he actually was. It was extremely gratifying to hear that he beat the odds. I thought if I were him, I'd go right out and buy a lottery ticket."

During the flight to Georges Bank the pilots were told to make a stop at Nantucket to pick up emergency medical technician Linda True of the Nantucket Fire Department. "I found out about the situation," remembers True, "when the fire chief rushed into my work area and said, 'Quick, we gotta go, the Coast Guard needs you.' We hopped in the chief's car and headed to the Coast Guard station. I figured I was going to be put on one of the Coast Guard patrol boats and brought to the injured man. When I got to the station, they took me to the men's room, handed me a dry suit, and said, 'Put this on.' Then the chief took me back to his car, and I said, 'What's going on here, aren't I getting on a boat?' And he said, 'Nope, a helicopter is picking you up and taking you out.'

"Thank God it was a beautiful, clear day because I'd never been in a helicopter. When we took off, I thought the helicopter would go straight up, but I was surprised how it went down the runway, slowly lifting. They put a headset on me, and they talked, probably to make me feel at ease, which I was."

Back on board the *Active*, Nicholson knew they'd have to wake Ernie, but he was reluctant to do so. "I knew he needed more medical care than we could give him. But I also could see that because of the big ocean swells, the helo wasn't going to be able to land safely on the cutter. Instead the survivor would have to be lifted by basket. Being lifted by a cable into the air is no picnic, and I was worried this might really put Ernie in shock!"

The crewman who had walked Ernie down to his sleeping quarters also felt bad about waking him up. Ernie had said all he needed was sleep and he'd be fine. The Coastie was also impressed that Ernie had kept his sense of humor. On the way to the deck they passed through a room where the floor had been recently waxed. Each time the ship took a wave the furniture in the room slid to the opposite side. The young Coastie said, "If you think this is bad, you should have been here yesterday." Ernie deadpanned back, "I would have liked that very much."

Ernie did not want to be airlifted off the boat. After spending more than two days on the open ocean he wasn't wild about being lashed into a basket supported by a single cable, then suspended above the seas he had so recently escaped. The corpsman sent for Tom McKenzie to help calm his patient.

"I remember," says McKenzie, "he was really pissed off about being forced to leave. He said something like 'I was just feeling better and just getting warm and now you're going to put me in a basket dangling above the ocean. That makes no sense.'

"There really wasn't much I could say," recalls McKenzie, "and I could certainly understand why he was mad. Imagine you just got out of the freezing cold ocean where you hadn't slept in three days. And just as you're finally starting to rest, we are going to put you in another scary situation. He was probably thinking, *I survived all of this only to risk getting killed by a basket dangling by a cable one hundred feet above the sea and ship.*"

Adding to Ernie's sour mood was a lifelong fear of heights. Now was not the time, he thought, to test his anxiety with a ride at the end of a swinging cable. McKenzie, however, informed him that he had no choice, and the two men walked onto the flight deck, where Ernie was given a coat and a life preserver.

Ernie shook his head in disgust. *How ironic*, he thought, *now that I'm safely aboard a ship, I'm being given a life jacket.* Then he heard the far-off drone of the helicopter and looked up to see it coming out of the western horizon.

Through the windshield of the helicopter, Linda True could see the *Active*'s white hull getting closer with each second. "When we got to the cutter I couldn't believe how big the waves were—the cutter was just going way up and then pounding back down. The man in the back started to get the basket ready. I said, 'You're not going to put me in that! You better bring that injured man to me.' There was no way I was going to get in that tiny basket. The pilot said, 'Don't worry, we're going to lower the basket and then bring the man up.' I got my gear ready and went in the back of the helicopter and waited for the injured man."

The cutter was turned so that it rode into the wind, and the helicopter turned in the same direction, approaching the ship from the stern. Winds buffeted the chopper like a kite, and Baley and Touzin struggled to hold position at the right distance from the rolling ship below. When Baley and Touzin had the helo at the appropriate height, they radioed the ship that they were ready and were lowering the basket.

The basket was just large enough for Ernie to sit in, and the corpsman and McKenzie helped Ernie inside, wrapping him in blankets. There was no chance for McKenzie to wish Ernie luck, so deafening was the roar from the helicopter. The corpsman signaled to the hoist operator that all was ready, and Ernie held on for dear life as the basket swung up and off the cutter's deck.

The two pilots did their best to keep the helicopter stable. If the basket swung too much or the helo bounced in the wind, they risked having Ernie swing so wildly that it would be difficult to pull him inside the big steel bird.

Ernie held the basket bars as tightly as he had the raft's inner straps during the height of the storm. He could see the cutter receding below him, and from above he was blasted by the turbulence of the whirling helicopter blades. He did not look up until he heard the metal clanging noise of the basket hitting the door of the helicopter. The hoist operator grabbed hold of the basket and guided it inside the door, and Ernie felt the basket rest on the floor of the helicopter.

The thundering rotors drowned out any chance for talking, but Ernie was in no mood anyway, especially with the helicopter's door wide open, causing him to feel vertigo and disorientation. He wanted to get as far into the helo as possible, and the hoist operator and Linda True helped him out of the basket and into a prone position.

———————◆———————

"I put a pair of headsets on Ernie so that we could communicate," says Linda. "I explained we were going to Cape Cod, and then he would be transferred to another helicopter and brought to a hospital in Beverly or Salem. His face and hands were really cold, and his feet were bright red and felt like ice. The captain of the cutter had radioed us about how he'd been in the raft for about forty-eight hours and how he was wet the whole time. I wondered how anyone could have survived. I checked his vital signs, and he was okay, and he was coherent, answering my questions with a word or two. I knew they had warmed him up on the cutter, and he'd had some soup, so perhaps the cold temperature of his extremities was primarily from being in the basket. But his feet were in bad shape probably due to lack of blood circulation. My primary concern was that he'd go into shock or maybe cardiac arrest. Every couple of minutes I'd ask him how he was feeling, and he always said fine. It was amazing that he never said a word about the discomfort he must have been in. We were flying to the mainland, and just before we got there I finally got him to talk a little more. He said, 'I'm okay, but I lost my buddies....They never had a chance.' I can remember thinking this is one brave man."

When the helicopter landed at Beverly Airport, a crowd had gathered. Among them were the loved ones of the missing crewmen, Ernie's brother and a friend, and the media. As Ernie was carried in a stretcher from the chopper to a waiting ambulance, reporters and photographers jostled one another for a closer look at the survivor.

Ernie shrank from the lights of the television cameramen and ignored the shouted questions of reporters. Just as he was placed in the ambulance, a newspaper photographer stuck his lens toward Ernie's face and snapped away. Ernie's brother Brent and neighbor Ron Michalak shooed the intruder away and climbed into the ambulance to accompany Ernie to the hospital.

Newspaper accounts of Ernie's ordeal appeared within hours. The *Salem Evening News* chronicled how "relatives of the missing crewmen were at the airport looking for a ray of hope." The *Boston Herald* spoke with Ron Michalak and ran a story with photos. Ernie was "in shock" and spoke little, said Michalak, who held Ernie's hands on the ride to the hospital. "It was the only communication necessary," the paper reported. That morning when he heard Ernie was alive, Michalak said, he "cried for ten minutes." Michalak's wife, Marilyn, said Ernie was like "an uncle" to their children. "You would not believe how many people love that man," she said.

"Ernie is a pretty rugged kid," Ron told the paper. "He has a love for the sea. He eats, sleeps and drinks lobster fishing." He added, "If I had to put money on somebody in a spot like that, it would be Ernie."

Chapter 27

A DIFFERENT KIND
OF PAIN

THE DOCTORS AT BEVERLY HOSPITAL WHO EXAM-
ined Ernie found him to be in remarkably good physical condition considering what he endured. They
found that frostbite had affected both his thighs,
where his flesh and tissue had actually frozen. Now
the thawed skin was red and painful.

Ernie's swollen feet, surprisingly, showed no signs
of frostbite, but he was diagnosed with a condition
known as immersion foot, a nonfreezing injury
occurring when the foot is submerged in water for a
long period of time. The malady is less severe than
frostbite because the tissue never actually freezes.

Still, Ernie's discolored feet now gave him a constant aching discomfort—even worse than when he was in the raft. But the medical prognosis was for a complete, or almost complete, recovery of his feet and thighs.

While the hospital labeled Ernie's physical condition as "good," his mental health was another matter. "He's very down," said hospital spokesman Jack Good. "He doesn't want to talk about it until he finds out about his shipmates."

The truth of the matter was that Ernie didn't want to talk about what happened unless it was to one of his crewmates' loved ones. Inside, he knew Billy, Rob, and Dave were dead, but he couldn't bring himself to say those words just yet.

Maria Pavlis learned from Coast Guard spokesman Captain Clyde Robbins that the search for Billy and the rest of the crew would resume on Tuesday. Robbins, however, had debriefed Ernie and was not optimistic that any other crew members had escaped the overturned *Fair Wind*, and he shared this assessment with the families. This came as no surprise to Maria.

She felt she knew Billy was gone the minute she first learned that Ernie was the only one inside the raft.

On Tuesday, Maria visited Ernie, wanting to give him comfort despite her own sorrow. She had spent the last two days with Billy's family, and when Billy's parents learned she was going to see Ernie, they too decided to go.

"When we saw Ernie in that hospital bed," says Maria, "we all broke down and cried. Ernie barely talked, he just kept squeezing our hands. We were all too choked up to talk, and it was obvious Ernie was physically and emotionally drained. It was all so emotional. On the one hand, we knew Billy and the others were gone, but on the other hand, we were just so happy Ernie was safe and was going to be all right."

Ernie wanted to comfort Maria and Billy's parents, but what could he say? The heartache he felt for them and for his lost crew was more extreme than his physical pain. He was experiencing the first pangs of survivor's guilt. *Why did I make it*, he wondered, *when the others did not, and so much of my survival depended on luck?* The question is a quite normal reaction to a traumatic event where others perish.

However, the survivor doesn't feel anywhere close to normal, but rather depressed and in jeopardy of falling into an abyss from which he cannot climb out. This was a new challenge the accident flung at Ernie. It was every bit as difficult to endure as the pounding of the seas and the trauma of hypothermia, frostbite, and immersion foot.

Ernie was overcome by two diametrically opposed emotions: gratitude for being alive and intense sorrow for the loss of his crewmates. In the raft, he had dreamed of a dry, warm bed, a steaming mug of coffee, and hours of uninterrupted sleep. Yet now that he had those things he simply could not allow himself to enjoy them fully. Instinctively, he knew that his ordeal was not over, and he steeled himself to be buffeted by strange and dark emotions. Just as he had in the raft, he would have to ride this out.

While Ernie lay in his hospital bed on Tuesday, *Fair Wind* owner Charlie Raymond was high above Georges Bank in a Coast Guard plane. With him was Dave Berry's father, George Berry, and Rob Thayer's uncle. Charlie scanned the ocean below with binoculars. Gone were the towering, cresting seas of the storm, replaced by an endless expanse of gray-green swells. Charlie knew it was a long shot that anyone would be found alive, but he had to look.

The plane that carried Charlie was joined in the search by several other Coast Guard planes, as well as a navy reconnaissance plane. Down below, the cutter *Active* conducted its own surface search, following the drift pattern that Ernie's raft had defined. None of the planes or the cutter spotted so much as a shred of debris from the missing vessel. The hunt continued all day, but by evening everyone knew that the *Fair Wind* and its remaining crew lay somewhere on the ocean floor, and the Coast Guard called off the search.

———

Ernie was released from the hospital on Wednesday, two days after his arrival, and looked forward to resting at his mother's house. Recuperation, however, was hard to come by because the phones were ringing almost constantly. Besides the calls of concern from friends and family, the Hazard home was deluged with calls from the media requesting interviews with Ernie. When Ernie refused, some reporters called back with offers of money. Still Ernie declined.

It was just too soon, and the last thing Ernie would do was profit from the deaths of his friends. However, when family members of the deceased crewmen called to learn the particulars of the accident and the storm, Ernie patiently retold the story. By now he had described the *Fair Wind*'s pitchpoling and his ensuing struggle several times, beginning back when he first arrived on the deck of the *Active*. And each time he told the story, it seemed as if a little bit of his soul was taken in the telling. But Ernie felt an obligation to explain to family members what had happened, just as he felt compelled to attend each of his friends' memorial services.

At the services, Ernie met the family members of the deceased and patiently answered their questions while battling a sense of shame for being alive while their sons, husbands, brothers were gone. He would explain that it was pure luck that he'd gotten out. He didn't tell them about the countless split-second decisions he had been forced to make. He also listened to some of the families venting their anger at the National Weather Service as details of the botched forecast and the malfunctioning weather buoys began to come to light.

Chapter 28

THE INQUIRY AND
A THANK-YOU

A WEEK AFTER THE ACCIDENT, THE COAST GUARD launched its official investigation, and Ernie was summoned to regional headquarters in Boston. His testimony filled several pages of the inquiry report. In addition to Ernie's testimony, Bob Brown and Charlie Raymond were questioned. The inquiry also took a closer look at the National Weather Service's forecasting. In the report, the Coast Guard marine safety commander, Harvey Knuth, stated, "It appears from this [testimony] that there is a definite discrepancy between the forecast and what the actual conditions were, at least what Ernie recalls. So at this point what I would like to do is contact the National Weather Service and give them an opportunity to testify regarding this discrepancy if they care to."

The National Weather Service responded by sending marine focal point meteorologist David Feit to testify. Feit had been working at the National Weather Service office at Logan Airport in Boston. He, along with fellow staff members, were responsible for issuing offshore marine forecasts that included the regions of the Gulf of Maine, Georges Bank, and south of Nova Scotia.

The Coast Guard commander asked Feit to describe the information used to make a forecast. Feit explained that besides obtaining on-scene information from ships in the region, "one of the main things we've been relying on over maybe the past five years or so have been buoys placed out there, including the one on Georges Bank. I have the coordinates in my file here. That one [the Georges Bank buoy] has not been operative for some months."

Feit went on to explain that an important function of the buoy is reporting wind direction speed on an hourly basis. "Had it been there and it would have given us perhaps that much of a jump" in the forecast.

The Coast Guard commander asked if Feit's office had made any effort to get these buoys back on line. Feit answered that indeed they had, writing several letters to the National Data Buoy Office "indicating we considered these buoys important input to our program and particularly with winter coming up we felt it was extremely important that they get these buoys in operation again."

Feit then voluntarily added, "I think there were certain inaccuracies in the forecast....The storm... did not go as far east as perhaps we expected. The intensity of the storm in terms of its pressure grading, which determines how fast the winds are going to be, was underestimated to some degree and the worst part of it was moved over [to the west at Georges Bank]. It's a question of accuracy and how well we can do given the science and the state of the science and the material and observations that are available to us."

As details of the Coast Guard inquiry were made public, some family members of the deceased concluded that the testimony confirmed that the weather report was inaccurate in part due to the faulty weather buoys. Later these family members and their attorney filed a lawsuit against the National Weather Service, the result of which made news across the country.

Ernie, however, wanted no part in any lawsuit. He was emotionally drained, and he wasn't interested in compensation. He worried that whatever he said about the accident could be twisted by lawyers and made to reflect poorly on Charlie Raymond or the *Fair Wind*. Ernie had told the story enough times and was well aware of the toll it was taking on him. He often felt that the months after the accident were as difficult as his fifty hours in the raft. Ernie removed himself from the controversy, and let his sense of gratitude guide his way.

———

About a month after the accident, Grant Moore was working down in the engine room of the *Broadbill*, which was docked in Fairhaven. He heard someone shout, "Is Grant Moore here?" Grant put down his greasy wrench, and as he climbed the stairs to the deck, he wondered who would be looking for him in the middle of winter. On deck Grant saw a man with a bushy black beard. The man introduced himself as Ernie Hazard.

"I just wanted to come down," said Ernie, "and thank you for what you did out there."

Grant doesn't remember if they said much more after that. "But it always stayed with me," says Grant, "that this man took the time to find me and thank me."

Ernie made one more stop: he tracked down Jim Givens at his office in Rhode Island and personally thanked him for building the raft that saved his life. After that, he did his best to get on with his life, keeping his *Fair Wind* buddies forever in his heart.

EPILOGUE

SEA-FEVER
—John Masefield

*I must go down to the sea again, to the
    lonely sea and the sky,
And all I ask is a tall ship and a star to
    steer her by,
And the wheel's kick and the wind's song
    and the white sail's shaking,
And a grey mist on the sea's face, and grey
    dawn breaking.*

*I must go down to the seas again, for the
    call of the running tide*

Is a wild call and a clear call that may not
be denied;
And all I ask is a windy day with the
white clouds flying,
And the flung spray and the blown spume,
and the sea-gulls crying.

I must go down to the seas again, to the
vagrant gypsy life,
To the gull's way and the whale's way
where the wind's like a whetted knife;
And all I ask is a merry yarn from a
laughing fellow-rover,
And quiet sleep and a sweet dream when
the long trick's over.

OVERLOOKING THE OCEAN IN FRONT OF THE LOB-
ster Pound store in the Manomet section of Plymouth,
Massachusetts, a portion of this poem is inscribed on
a plaque fitted into a memorial stone in memory of
Gary Brown. Honour Brown, Gary's wife, had the
stone placed there. The poem was also read at Billy
Garnos's service.

After the accident Ernie took some time off. In the spring of 1981 he was looking for a peaceful environment to work in, and he found it as a maintenance worker, in a cemetery of all places. "It was a beautiful place—rolling lawns, flowers, a lake. So for a few months I used equipment to dig graves and maintain the cemetery."

Later in 1981 Ernie left the cemetery job and drove out to California to visit friends in Carmel. He decided to stay in the area doing odd jobs until the lure of the sea called, and he was hired as a deckhand on a fishing boat out of Monterey. Ernie did not feel any trepidation about returning to the sea, and he needed a steady paycheck. This vessel was a similar size as the *Fair Wind* and made day trips about ten miles offshore to fish for black cod.

"I later learned," says Ernie, "that the guy I replaced on the boat died at sea when he got tangled in the gear and dragged over. And about the same time I also lost one of my best friends at sea. He was in a skiff on a calm day, and somehow it flipped over, and he drowned. I was beginning to wonder if it was somehow payback for me surviving the raft ride."

Ernie eventually left commercial fishing but stayed in California. Reflecting on the November 1980 storm, he thinks that the experience of the crew of the *Sea Fever* was no less difficult than his own. "I marveled how Peter and his crew kept that flooded boat afloat. No windshields, a damaged pilothouse, losing a man overboard—Peter sure had a lot on his plate."

———

One might think that spending more than forty-eight hours on the brink between life and death would cause radical changes in behavior, but for Ernie the change was more subtle. "There's no reason for me to be here, so I figure what the heck. Since the storm hit around Thanksgiving, I tend to think that's my real birthday, my second life. These are free years I'm living. And so I don't let little stuff get to me. And when bigger problems come along, I figure I'll solve them somehow. I am surely thankful for each and every day. Everyone involved in that storm is in my mind all the time, every day.

"My life has been incredible. I've met so many

fascinating people—some important, some famous, and some just special. And I appreciate the little things. Each day I take the long way to work, just to see the beauty of the coast. It's hard to say if this appreciation is from the raft experience or just the way I am now...maybe a little of both."

When asked if Ernie thought God saved him because he had plans for him, Ernie joked, "I think God was too busy to take on my problems. Maybe I was spared to keep me out of his hair."

APPENDIX

The Court Case: Brown v. United States

The families of Billy Garnos, Dave Berry, and Gary Brown filed a lawsuit charging the National Weather Service with negligence and asking for $3.2 million in damages. After a seven-day, nonjury trial in May 1984, US District Court Judge Joseph Tauro ruled for the plaintiffs that the federal government was liable, and he awarded the families $1.2 million in total damages.

This was the first time in the history of the United States that the National Weather Service was found responsible for an inaccurate forecast. Judge Tauro said government negligence in issuing the forecast was a "substantial factor" in the deaths of the fishermen. The ruling was featured in newspapers across the country and spawned articles both for and against the decision, many with simplistic but eye-catching headlines such as "Weatherman Is Found Guilty." The lawsuit, however, was quite complex, and at its heart was the government's failure to repair or replace the malfunctioning weather buoys.

But the ruling did not stand for long. In 1986 the US First Circuit Court of Appeals reversed the judgment. The appeals court said the government is protected from liability because the act of weather forecasting is a discretionary function for which the US government cannot be held liable as outlined in the Federal Tort Claims Act.

AUTHOR'S NOTE

If I'm going to devote two or three years to researching and writing a story, the event has got to grab me, shake me, and ultimately make me so curious that I just can't let go. But having a burning interest isn't enough—the people related to the event have to be open, honest, and kind enough to carefully answer my questions. And so I felt lucky that the first person I contacted was Sarge (Richard Rowell). I called Sarge first simply because he was the only one of the survivors I could find when searching an online directory for Massachusetts. After I explained why I was calling, I waited for his response, knowing it could be guarded, vague, or even curt. Instead we immediately fell into a comfortable conversation, and with that first phone call I was off and running.

I explained to Sarge that I had come across the story of the *Sea Fever* and the *Fair Wind* while performing research for my book *Ten Hours Until Dawn*. I asked him if he thought he could help me track down the other men. Sarge said he could definitely put me in touch with Brad and Peter, but he didn't know what had happened to Ernie Hazard. I felt a little of the wind go out of my sails, knowing that without Ernie there could be no book. Then Sarge said that if anyone knew what happened to Ernie it would be the owner of the *Fair Wind*, Charlie Raymond. Sarge gave me Charlie Raymond's phone number and encouraged me to call him.

Sure enough Charlie was helpful and said that although he had not seen Ernie in years, he thought that Ernie had moved to California. I quickly found Ernie's telephone number, but before calling, I tracked down additional information about the event. I first went through various 1980 editions of local newspapers, reading about the storm, the boats involved, and how the Coast Guard responded to so many Maydays. These write-ups, in addition to the marine casualty report, gave me a good overview of what had transpired out at Georges Bank, and I now felt I could at least call Ernie and be conversant with some of the details.

A week later I spoke to Ernie on a Sunday afternoon, explaining that I found his story absolutely amazing and thought it needed to be told in its entirety. I asked him a few questions, and after just five minutes of talking I knew he was just the kind of man I wanted to work with. No pretense, no ego, just a directness that I found refreshing. I told him about the little bit of research I'd done, and explained that I wanted to fly out to California and interview him in person. We decided I'd visit in three months, in May. In the meantime, Ernie did me a huge favor by mailing me a thick package of information about the accident and his survival.

When May came, I called Ernie to find out what days were best to visit. He invited me to stay at his house, and I took him up on his offer. I figured we'd need at least two or three days to go over all the material, and I decided to spend almost a full week in California. I'm glad I did. I had one of the most interesting weeks of my life.

I conducted the interview with Ernie in a marathon session starting the evening of my first day and then continuing through the next two days. How this man sat so patiently and answered all my questions was in itself a minor miracle. When we were through, I felt like I'd been a fellow crewman aboard the *Fair Wind*. Ernie's explanations were so complete, I believed I had everything I needed.

When I returned to Massachusetts, I tracked down Grant Moore and interviewed him in the pilothouse of his newer eighty-foot lobster boat. Then over the next couple of months I conducted individual interviews with Sarge, Peter Brown, and Brad Bowen. Just like Ernie, they never tried to make themselves sound brave or felt the need to embellish. Equally important, each man's memories of the events matched the others'. To be sure, they felt different emotions at different times, and each had his own perspective in hindsight, but their recollections of a myriad of facts all matched perfectly.

After I talked with these key people I took a break from the interviewing process and focused on the wealth of information that was chronicled in the depositions and testimony during the lawsuit against the National Weather Service. I found this material at the National Archives in Waltham, Massachusetts.

Upon exhausting the National Archives I turned my attention to the men and women from the Coast

Guard who were involved in the storm. I first interviewed many of the Coasties on the *Active* who remembered the search and the storm. Then I talked with the pilot and copilot of the helicopter that made the dangerous flight into the storm to assist the *Sea Fever*. Buck Baley and Joe Touzin patiently walked me through their activities during the flight and explained what they were thinking and feeling during the nighttime mission.

Of all the meetings I had with people involved in the story, my evening with Maria Pavlis was one of the most memorable. Charming and thoughtful, she gave the story a different perspective, of what it was like to be back on land and hearing—in agonizing bits of news—about the tragedy that had unfolded offshore.

Researching the ordeal that the men of the *Fair Wind* and *Sea Fever* went through has not changed my love of the ocean, but it has increased my respect and wariness. I still go fishing for striped bass every chance I get and still take my kayak out to fish or ride the waves. In fact, my proximity to the ocean probably helped me write the book because I wrote the chapter about the pitchpoling of the *Fair Wind* and the blown windows of the *Sea Fever* when I was renting a cottage overlooking the ocean on Cape Cod in October. A two-day storm slammed the Cape while I was there. Between sessions of writing on my computer I waded out into the surf and cast for striped bass. The roar of the wind and the crashing of the waves were probably only 1 percent of the decibel level that assaulted Ernie, but it certainly helped me appreciate the sudden power and fury of the sea.

It was during that weeklong writing sojourn on Cape Cod that I reread my notes from my meeting with Ernie. I tried to put myself in his place while he was in the raft, facing mountainous waves and extreme cold. The more I thought of what he endured, the decisions he made, and the steely outlook he developed, the more I realized how truly unique a human being he is. Ernie would disagree, of course, saying he was lucky and did what anyone else would try to do, but I know better.

I like to think that when I undertook this book I had a big, blank canvas in front of me, and the only way it could be painted was through interviewing the people involved in the storm. Each person contributed, painted his or her section of the canvas, and I was the lucky one who got to put my name on the bottom. But it's their painting, their story, and for their help I am forever grateful.

ACKNOWLEDGMENTS

My thanks to all the survivors and rescuers who took the time to answer my many questions about their experiences chronicled in *Fatal Forecast*. And my deep appreciation for editor and publisher Christy Ottaviano—she is the best in the business!

To read an excerpt of *Abandon Ship! The True World War II Story About the Sinking of the* Laconia, also by Michael J. Tougias, please turn the page....

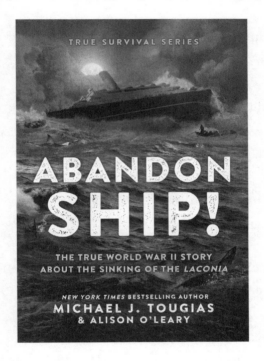

"This epic story races along, unspooling like a movie before our eyes.... An intriguing book."

—DOUG STANTON, #1 *New York Times* bestselling author of *In Harm's Way*

"Ideal for WWII history fans and readers who have graduated from Lauren Tarshis's 'I Survived' series."
—*SCHOOL LIBRARY JOURNAL*

"A gripping wartime story that probes moral uncertainties."
—*KIRKUS REVIEWS*

"The authors do an excellent job of conveying the chaos and loss of this grisly historical incident without pushing young readers too deeply into the horror.... Archival photos add immediacy to this sensational true-life story."
—*THE WALL STREET JOURNAL*

"An amazing account of a World War II event that is almost entirely unknown."
—*BOOKLIST*

"[A] pulse-pounding work."
—*PUBLISHERS WEEKLY*

A HARSH PENALTY

TONY LARGE, LIFEBOAT #2
Approximately September 24–30

AROUND THE EIGHTH OR NINTH DAY ADRIFT SINCE the bombing of U-156, eight men died in Tony's lifeboat within twenty-four hours. Now just twenty-two men were left from the original fifty-one.

With so many gone, the remaining survivors had enough room to stretch out and lie down. And with fewer men in the boat the fresh water supply didn't shrink as rapidly.

One night, near the end of September, Tony was awakened by shouts. He sat up in the dim light of the rising moon and looked where a survivor was pointing. A freighter was steaming perpendicular to the lifeboat, a mere three hundred to four hundred yards away!

The survivors shouted and blew their lone whistle. The freighter did not slow down. Someone picked up the axe and pounded it against the steel hull of the lifeboat, sending loud bangs reverberating into the night. Surely a lookout on the ship would hear the blows.

Still the ship kept moving. Survivors were screaming and shouting, but no one on the ship heard their cries, and the vessel disappeared into the darkness.

To have salvation so close and have nothing come of it was a crushing blow. One minute survivors were filled with fresh hope and the next they sank into despair. The incident broke the spirit of several men, and they were dead within a day. Others soon succumbed to the deadly practice of drinking seawater, and they too perished.

Tony was overcome by misery and dejection, but his inner strength would not allow him to give up. He vowed to fight on until his last breath.

———◆———

The passing ship not only crushed the resolve of some men to live, it made one survivor do something that was unpardonable. A young soldier with an angular face was accused of sneaking a drink from the lone water canister. The soldier vigorously denied the charges of this ultimate betrayal. Tony had not seen the alleged incident, but he and the others warned the soldier that if he or any survivor was found stealing—or even meddling with the water can—the penalty would be severe. They would be tossed overboard.

Despite the warning, the next day the same young man was caught in the act. He was using a piece of rubber tubing: one end was in the water can and the other in his mouth. This time the soldier did not deny it. He knew his fate. He said he was sorry, took a big drink of seawater, and administered the penalty to himself by stepping over the side of the boat and swimming away.

The remaining survivors watched him go. No one said a word.

———◉———

Every hour, every death, and every event that would be impossible to imagine in the civilized world was wearing Tony down. He did not think it could get worse. But it did.

Tony had formed a friendship with a Canadian air force officer whom he called Canada. He was a gentle and considerate soul, and prior to their tongues becoming too swollen and dry to talk, the two men had commiserated together and had gotten to know each other. Or so Tony thought.

Just a day or two after the close encounter with the ship, one of the survivors shouted, "Look, Canada!"

Tony glanced up and saw Canada calmly slip over the side of the boat and paddle away, never looking back, never saying a word.

For the first time in this nightmare Tony sobbed uncontrollably. He could do nothing to save his friend.

CREEPING MADNESS

JIM MCLOUGHLIN AND DORIS HAWKINS,
LIFEBOAT #1

Approximately September 26–October 2

It almost seemed inevitable that some cast-aways on Jim and Doris's lifeboat would resort to drinking seawater, as they had on Tony's vessel. The thirst tormented them so much that it overruled sound decision-making. Despite warnings from Jim, Doris, and Dr. Purslow, a few of the survivors began this desperate act. Within hours they were talking gibberish or rambling nonsense about things only they could see.

Listening to these men put Doris in a dark place, and she tried to shut out the noise, afraid it would cause her to lose her ability to reason. She was suffering more than ever and forcing herself to eat her one mouthful of food per day. It took her an hour just to swallow a tiny bit of pemmican.

One of the men, Zdzislaw Uher, was able to eat a biscuit every day by dipping it in seawater to soften it, and suffered no harm from the practice. Doris did not want to take such a risk, but she was thankful when this same man had enough strength during the heat of the day to dip a canister into the ocean and pour the water over Doris's head for a bit of relief.

———◈———

Jim knew that each day the number of people in the lifeboat diminished because of deaths. But now he wondered if some of the scuffling he heard during the night were the noises of the strong throwing one of the weak overboard so that the drinking water would last longer. He wasn't sure, but he tried to project strength—he did not want to look like one of the weak.

Jim's hunch was correct. Another survivor on his boat, Harold Gibson, later explained that the healthier men knew who was going to die next. He said he could tell who was going to die by their eyes. "Eyes tell you a lot. When they look at you with sad eyes they know they are dying. In fact some were wishing to die."

Gibson explained that in an effort to conserve drinking water some of the men decided to throw the weakest overboard while they were still alive. "We knew in our hearts they were going to be dead the next day so we just ditched them over the side and saved the water for those that were strong enough."

Was this act murder? Was it justified by the horrific conditions? Was Gibson trying to excuse his actions by saying "some were wishing to die"? Those questions are simply too difficult to answer. But Jim's determination to look strong was well-founded. He would not be sacrificed to the ocean so others could have more drinking water.

One night Jim lay awake in the bow, looking back toward the stern and saw the man who was controlling the tiller suddenly stand up and start singing.

"Show me the way to go home!" the man sang. "I'm tired and I want to go to bed."

Jim's eyes widened, terrified of what the man might do next. Like the words in the song it was likely the man did in fact take a drink, not of alcohol, but seawater. Another possibility was that he broke the lifeboat's compass, which was later found in pieces. Inside the compass was a tiny amount of alcohol that he might have drunk. Perhaps he drank both the alcohol and seawater. Whatever the reason, his thoughts were a jumbled mess.

The man sang another line or two and then, without any notice, jumped overboard.

Jim was shaken to the core that delirium was creeping through the boat. He could hear the man in the water still singing at the top of his lungs as he drifted away from the boat.

Jim started to fear each night. Adding to the gloom and eerie feeling was the phosphorescence—the glowing plankton—that twinkled in the wake of the slow-moving vessel. Jim felt like he was no longer on earth but in the spirit world, and he worried he was losing his own mind. He stayed at the bow of the vessel and rarely slept.

With the compass broken, the survivors had to navigate by the sun during the day and the stars at night. This was not as precise as using the compass, and some questioned if the navigation was getting them closer to shore. Like in Tony's lifeboat, a couple of men didn't wait for death to take them but simply crawled to the side of the vessel as they gave up hope altogether.

Both Jim and Doris fought to keep a grip on their emotions. The days were all blending together, and they no longer kept track of how long they had been adrift.

<hr>

About two weeks into their terrible odyssey there was reason for hope. While staring out at the ocean, trying yet again to appreciate its ever-changing hues of greens, blues, and grays, Doris saw something on the horizon. Her eyes were dry and stinging from the lack of moisture and the glare of the sun, but she squinted, and on the crest of a small wave she saw the object again.

"Ship!" she croaked.

People who had the strength to sit up also saw the vessel. They shouted and waved, and one man even produced a whistle that he blew as loud as he could.

But the ship, a three-funnel vessel, was approximately four miles away. This was the opportunity they had all been waiting for, and they had to get the attention of the sailors on the ship. Using a cigarette lighter, which miraculously still functioned, they set fire to a life jacket, placed it in a bucket and held it aloft. Black smoke wafted into the air.

Doris prayed. *Surely the ship is turning*, she thought. Craning forward, she watched hopefully. *No, not yet.*

One of the men in the bow exclaimed, "She is nearer!"

Jim, shielding his eyes from the sun, thought it did appear the ship was getting nearer.

"That's the *Britannic*," Jim said, eyes fixed on the horizon. "She was in Cape Town when *Laconia* called in there. I remember her shape. A liner. A Cunard White Star ship."

Doris, Jim, and many of the others were now convinced rescue was imminent. Some talked of the food and the rum they would soon consume aboard the ship.

They waited. And waited. The ship kept moving at a steady pace. The man in the bow was wrong: the ship was not coming closer, nor had its lookout seen the lifeboat from such a distance.

Doris slumped back on the deck, feeling overwhelming despair.

One of the sailors muttered, "She didn't bloody well stop."

Jim responded that the men on the ship never saw the lifeboat. "We're a tiny boat low down in the water. It would've been a miracle if she'd seen us."

Having potential rescue so close and not come to fruition absolutely devastated the morale on the lifeboat. For some, this was a turning point, the time when they lost their will to live. It seemed that fate had conspired against them and that they were doomed to suffer alone on the endless sea. Once hope was gone, it was hard to carry on the fight.

One of the older officers tried to improve the group's spirits, saying, "We've had a big disappointment today, but there's always tomorrow. The fact that we have seen a ship means we are near a shipping route, and perhaps our luck will turn now."

But when another day went by with no ship in sight, more people lost hope and passed away.

Doris and Jim rallied from their despair and renewed their belief that somehow they would be saved. Doris and a couple of men led the group in prayer at night. They would need a miracle, fate, or incredible good luck to survive.

Lindsey Potter

MICHAEL J. TOUGIAS is the author of *Abandon Ship!*, which he cowrote with Alison O'Leary, and many other award-winning true rescue stories, including the *New York Times* bestseller *The Finest Hours, A Storm Too Soon, Into the Blizzard, Rescue of the Bounty,* and *Attacked at Sea,* as well as the young reader's adaptation of *In Harm's Way* by Doug Stanton. A frequent lecturer who also enjoys visiting schools to talk about his books and show slides from the stories, Tougias splits his time between Massachusetts and Florida. He invites you to visit him online at michaeltougias.com.